The A-Z
of Cheaper Boating

A Practical Guide

Bill Beavis

Illustrated by Alan Roy

Stanley Paul, London

Stanley Paul & Co Ltd
3 Fitzroy Square, London W1P 6JD

An imprint of the Hutchinson Publishing Group

London Melbourne Sydney Auckland
Wellington Johannesburg and agencies
throughout the world

First published 1977
© Bill Beavis 1977
Drawings © Stanley Paul & Co Ltd 1977

Set in Monotype Times

Printed in Great Britain by The Anchor Press Ltd
and bound by Wm Brendon & Son Ltd, both of
Tiptree, Essex

ISBN 0 09 129060 0 (cased)
       0 09 129061 9 (paperback)

10.95

The A-Z of Cheaper Boating

By the same author

Plain Sailing
Modern Rope Seamanship (with Colin Jarman)
Under Weigh

Contents

Acknowledgements

I should like to say thank you to these kind people without whose help this book would not have been possible. I should also like to thank all the anonymous people whose brains I've picked, many of whom might see their ideas repeated here, and finally thank all those of the yachting trade who answered my letters.

Edward Blundell; Ted Broadhurst; Bill Colles; Denny Desoutter, editor of *Practical Boatowner*; Gerald Dunkerley MA; Christopher Emmet of the Arun Yacht Club; Mr H. E. Evans; John Farr MA; Paul Gartside; Loris Goring; Gerald Hammond; Gudmund F. Jorgensen; Andre Kanssen of the Amateur Yacht Research Society; Mr F. A. Menice; David Newton-Crum; Bill Robertson, president of the Roa Island Boating Club; Mrs Rona Roy; Mrs Sally Sargeaunt; Des Sleightholme, editor of *Yachting Monthly*; Geoffrey Smyth AA Dipl. RIBA; John Teal, naval architect; Graham Watts.

Introduction

Twenty years ago there lived a simple old man with a simple wooden boat. It had a sail, a rudder, a bucket to bail her and, for those windless days, a pair of oars to bring her back. The boat was kept at the head of a creek and two or three times a week, on warm summer evenings, the old man would come down for a sail. He maintained the boat himself, and he knew her capabilities and her limitations. He also knew all about tides and weather and was, altogether, a very competent, unsophisticated man.

Then they built a marina in the creek and thousands of new folk from the city were able to take up sailing. They were keen and impatient and decided that the object of this new sport must be competition. And competition in all things, in the size of the boat, in comfort, in equipment, and speed of course – they bought hundreds of go-fast gadgets – even competition in the kind of clothes they bought. Perhaps that's why they ignored the old chap in his grey flannel trousers and his wellington boots. He wasn't the kind of star they wanted to follow.

Then sadly their supply of money began to dry up and there wasn't a lot left over for luxuries like sailing. Desperate that their new boats might have to go they turned to the old man to help them.

'How is it,' they shouted across the creek, 'how is it an old pauper like you can run a boat when the FT Index keeps falling?'

But he didn't hear them – he was gone, poor devil. Some go-fast gadget had collapsed under strain, came cannonballing up the creek and picked him off as a target!

This book, however, is not a call for his resurrection, nor is it a suggestion that we should all make the great leap backwards! Primitive things may be all fine and noble but modern technology is here to stay and we might as well reap the harvest. No, I only related this sorry tale because in a fast-changing sport where the base level seems ever to spiral and the beginner never knows where to start – let alone whether he will be able to afford it – that old chap serves as a reminder – a reminder that after all is said and done this is a pastime that concerns a man and his boat on the water. It's the safe and skilful handling of that boat and just being afloat that brings the man his pleasure; all else is incidental.

I am concerned that not only has boating become much too expensive, and far more than it need be, but that it is not so carefree and relaxing as it once was. I don't see how, with so many new things aboard to worry us, we can possibly derive the same pleasure. Take the proliferation of instruments for example. They shoulder much of this responsibility.

When I went to sea it was the period of history which is now judged to be the dawning of marine electronics. Not that I was ever aware of it, the mean Scottish outfit that I sailed in being stuck in the previous sunset. So it happened that by the time I finally joined a modern, fully instrumented ship, a new order had been established, new attitudes firmly entrenched and the dust of the revolution well settled. I, on the other hand, still had the dank smell of the *ancien régime*. The captain said as much. Having seen me trying to double-the-angle-on-the-bow on the bridge of his 25-knot, 100000-ton ship, he commented that it was like having someone come back from the dead.

Needless to say, the other watchkeepers didn't do things this way; they used the automatic plotter. And while it took me just about the entire watch to keep permanent check on where we were, peering through sextants, taking bearings, soundings and working endless computations on scraps of paper, they had the position fixed in a matter of moments.

Then one night after I had been long delayed trying to find where we were – more mysticism than science that night I remember – my 'relief' came in from the wing of the bridge and re-directed his mindless gaze at my workings.

'D'you know,' he said when he finally finished yawning, 'I really believe you enjoy navigation.'

Instruments are one explanation of the spiralling costs, gadgets are another. And especially gadgets and other things that sell under the imprint of that holiest of holies: safety. If something is held to improve safety, then the newcomer to the sport feels conscience-bound to buy it. What a lot of silly hypocrisy this is! A nation that over-eats, over-drinks, smokes, takes millions of unproven pills and very little exercise should worry its miserable self about *safety*.

Perhaps if there were less safety gear and facilities around people would take more care of themselves and rely on their own resources; make sure that their boats were sound and well maintained and their knowledge of a comparable standard. You wouldn't need to legislate as the old gut fear makes a fine disciplinarian.

And let's not pay too much heed to that emotive rejoinder about putting 'brave lives' at risk. The man who knows what he's doing doesn't usually need a lifeboat. I study the figures every year and it's the mechanical breakdowns that consistently top the bill, those and the people who see the RNLI as a get-you-home service.

Another area for economy, although this more particularly concerns the home-builder, is that too much emphasis is laid on making a yacht look pretty. Compare her with a working boat. Would you say that a fishing smack was any less attractive? And yet look at the latter's massive sections, rubbing bands, gunwales and general absence of brightwork and frills.

For some crazy reason yachts are built to delight their owner's vanity and decorative sense and yet spend ninety per cent of their time out of his vision. And not carefully parked in a garage mind you but on the water rubbing shoulders with all the riff-raff, or getting hammered by a gale on the mooring. If yachts were built for the conditions and the places they inhabit, they would cost considerably less to build and save a small fortune in repairs. The majority of insurance claims for damage originate while the boat is unattended at a berth or on a mooring.

Perhaps the most irritating of all the unnecessary and superfluous features about modern boats and boating is the recent invasion by the plastic knick-knack industry. Pretty soon, if things continue, we won't be able to recognize the old seamanlike, commonsense way of doing things. Indeed there are signs that it's happening already.

'I'm sure you *could* do that,' said one man to me when I explained the usual way to stop crockery skidding was to place it on a wet dishcloth, 'but don't you know you can buy the *proper*, non-slip rubber mats nowadays?'

On another occasion I presided over a long-winded argument about the perfidy of a certain nylon guardrail connector. It seemed almost fatuous to point out that had rope lashing been used the argument would never have started, and the leading protagonist never have gone overboard.

So here we are struggling to keep our boats going through these hard times and yet all the while being hit by the temptations of expensive fashion and work-making conformity. What I have tried to do in this book is to help you beat them off. To ensure you walk a sensible, solvent path and keep your wife off the streets and your kids out of 'care'. To remind you too that, like the man in the creek, quite ordinary folk have always had boats, long before the sport was taken up by the idle and decadent Edwardians or the 'Leisure Division' of the Acme Investment Corporation.

The book is set out in alphabetical order and the idea of this is that should you plan to make a change or buy something new you might like to look up the relevant feature or item within the book and consider a commonsense, seamanlike – even frugal – but guaranteed cheaper alternative.

Finally, there hasn't been the space to provide working drawings or even the full details of some of the inspired DIY creations so here and there you will find the references of where they have appeared in yachting magazines. If you take this reference to the local library they will be able to send away for photostat copies.

Advertise For every man desperately in need of a cooker, an anchor, a winch or some other item of deck machinery there is a wife somewhere even more desperate to clear one from the attic, the garage or the outside loo. Advertise in the 'Wanted' column of the local newspaper and you may well connect. It should be specifically the small local paper because they sell largely on their classified pages and their advertising charges are much less.

Anchor If you customarily anchor over rocks or other people's moorings and have on occasion lost or fouled your anchor then try the old fishermen's dodge of anchoring to a bag of sand – as a temporary measure anyway. A bag of sand may sound a needlessly heavy item to carry around but sand can have other uses like mopping up oil spills, as a fire extinguisher or a dirt box for the cat (*see also* BALLAST). It's an old trick also to to carry a bag of sand under the forefoot when running into shallow water – particularly at night – when the sudden bump as the bag strikes the bottom not only gives warning of decreasing depth but also brings the boat up and prevents her from grounding. No scratches or hull damage are incurred with a bag of sand.

Figure 1

An alternative to the bag of sand as an extempory anchor is a small hook made from a piece of 1 inch (25mm) water pipe (Figure 1). It is effective when anchoring over reeds or thick seaweed which the sandbag cannot penetrate. Two short lengths of steel rod are driven through holes in the pipe and form a snug fit.

Anchor winch This heavy, space-taking and expensive item can be dispensed with altogether if you use – (*a*) a nylon warp, (*b*) a chain pawl, or (*c*) a snubber. The advantages of the nylon warp are discussed under CABLE so let's move on to the pawl (Figure 2).

Figure 2   Figure 3

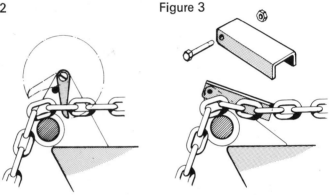

This was invented by the Victorian yachtsman Claude Worth. As the cable is hauled aboard, the pawl trips over the links and engages so as to stop them running back; not only does it enable you to rest between hauling but it can also be made to do the heavy work. Hold the cable fast while the bow moves upwards with the force of the wave. Then as the bow drops the cable goes slack and you can take in. The pawl is lifted when the anchor is let go and similarly when the anchor is made fast. The boat must never be allowed to ride on the pawl. The standard stem roller fitting can be adapted to take a pawl (see Figure 3).

The snubber (Figure 4) is merely a hardwood block bolted through the deck to a pad below. It is notched and stiffened at

16

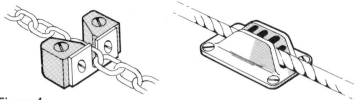

Figure 4

the back by a galvanized or brass plate, and notched to correspond with the thickness of chain. The snubber works on exactly the same principle as the pawl in that it takes on the heavy work; a camcleat can be used for rope.

Anti-fouling   A well known paint company had a sales drive in Cornwall but when they came to sell their expensive anti-fouling to fishermen they met with little success. The fishermen preferred a concoction of their own. A sample of this was taken away to the company's laboratories, tested and found to be remarkably effective. The ingredients? Creosote, Jeyes' fluid and seagull eggs.

Ex-Navy anti-fouling paints can sometimes be bought and users claim that these give satisfactory results on GRP hulls; for wooden boats it is claimed that bitumen-based paints sold as damp-proof remedies have anti-fouling properties.

Asking price   It is customary, when a man comes to sell his boat, to increase the price by the amount he thinks he'll have to climb down. It sounds nonsensical and it is, but the practice has only come about because buyers traditionally try to beat the poor chap down. Don't forget then, when buying a boat, to keep up the tradition and go for a figure that is 5 per cent less than the *asking price*. That you should find is just about the boat's true value.

Auctions   It has been suggested that the best time to attend an auction is when a televised cup final coincides with a wet Saturday, which usually results in a dramatic reduction in the numbers of bidders. Auctions are a good source of second-hand boats and equipment but do check well before bidding because you will not be able to argue about condition after the sale. Ideally boats should be surveyed. Auction dates and venues are usually announced in the small ad. section of yachting magazines.

AYRS The Amateur Yacht Research Society (AYRS) is a fine and almost free source of information on any problem which the home-builder or designer is likely to meet. Members are prolific writers, communicating their ideas and experiments on design, construction, sails, rigging and equipment in booklets and magazines. The society has done a tremendous amount to further the development of low-cost sailing and equipment as well as producing some entirely new concepts. Three best-selling books have also been published on the practical consideration of rudder design, speed sailing and self-steering. For membership write to: Michael Ellison, AYRS, Hermitage, Newbury, Berks.

Ballast, metal It takes you aback to enter a scrapyard and see the 'guv'nor' sat down, strings tied round his trousers and a copy of the *Financial Times* on his lap. But he is of course studying the current mineral prices and if you have come to buy lead you should do the same. The price of lead can fluctuate quite remarkably.

But rather than pay the market price collect items of lead over a period of time and smelt them down into pigs. Lead can sometimes be bought cheaper as old pipes and flashing from demolition sites when the absence of a set of scales usually results in a more favourable deal for the buyer. Lead can also be got from old car or truck batteries: use salt to kill the acid. Or contact your local roofing tiler. He collects a quantity of lead and traditionally sells it at Christmas for his bonus. A well-timed telephone call could fill your stocking as well.

Boiler punchings and sash weights are popular ballast materials. The cheapest way to collect sash weights is to contact the borough engineer of a town where slum clearance has been going on. (When I told the man I needed a ton and a half, he said, 'Good heavens, that's about six bloody streetfulls!') Sash weights are currently about £25 per ton. Ballast of this type needs to be firmly concreted into the bilge otherwise, should the boat capsize, it is likely to rain down on your head.

Remember also that this sort of iron or steel ballast material is magnetic so keep a check on your compass.

Ballast, sand   Not only is sand a cheap form of internal ballast but it is so adaptable as well. Stowed in strong fertilizer bags it snugs down well in all kinds of awkward corners and doesn't need to be secured as solid ballast does. It makes ideal trimming ballast. Time was when every boat carried trimming ballast to be lugged forward or aft to compensate heavy weights in the cockpit, or empty fuel tanks. A few bags of sand properly placed can produce an appreciable increase in speed. Then again sand ballast is useful as a weight on deck, either to heel the vessel on the desired side when taking the ground or to trim her when touching up the waterline or carrying out repairs, or even to jettison overboard to lighten ship when you've gone aground. (*See also* ANCHOR.)

Barograph   Well not exactly a barograph but you get the same results. Every hour, or every time you change watch, plot the barometer reading on to a sheet of barograph paper and then join up the points. It gives you the same graphic record of pressure and does away with the diurnal curve. If you cannot get hold of barograph paper use ordinary squared paper and mark off pressure units and hours.

Beachcombing   Good contemplative exercise with the serendipity that you might find something good for the boat. In twelve months of regular walks on the beach I collected a full set of fenders, a full set of sail battens, buckets, bailers, anchor buoys, a huge quantity of rope and hardwood, several stainless steel and bronze fittings that were screwed on to various things, two sail bags and fifty-eight rubber flip-flops, none of which matched up.

Berthing charges   For every swank marina or crowded harbour charging a pound or two for the night there are a dozen free places to anchor. Personally, I can think of nothing more miserable than to lie double-banked for the night with squeaking fenders, rattling halyards and drunks rolling back to announce themselves 'Strangers in Paradise'. Much more civilized to anchor outside along with the fishes and the birds.

Unfortunately, many of us have got out of the way of using our anchors – and a good many more have never tried. Practise anchoring so that when the opportunity presents itself you can do so with confidence and sleep better for it through the night – in settled conditions even row ashore if you like.

Anchoring in a creek or river is fairly straightforward, even taking the ground for the night, but remember one can also spend a very peaceful night anchored in a lee in the bay. Finding a lee is the thing, a headland, or a sandbank which nearly uncovers, something to take the sting out of the wind and dampen the waves. Obviously you will only do this in favourable weather; if there is a chance of a wind increase then have a plan of escape worked out, a harbour of refuge to run to perhaps. When looking for an anchorage have a large-scale chart, and use the leadline to tell you how well the sea bed will hold your anchor. Sand is plainly observed stuck to the tallow and so is gravel or shale, but if the lead comes up clean then this suggests rocks, weed or pebbles and not such a good spot to anchor in. Keep a record of the anchorages you find by noting the shore bearings in case you wish to go there again.

Blocks There is more than one yacht sailing today with its running gear set by courtesy of the army and navy stores; heavy and unattractive though it might be, the galvanized pulley customarily sold to housewives for washing lines is a perfectly adequate piece of equipment. In any event if you carry a 'handy billy' aboard, and every boat should have this simple tackle, then certainly make this up with galvanized pulleys; tufnol blocks for a job like this are merely an extravagance.

Aerial insulators make reasonable, near-frictionless blocks and although perhaps not entirely suited for rigging they can be made up into a useful tackle whenever that extra purchase is needed.

20

Rope-stropped blocks

The rope-stropped block can either be made up with the conventional rope grommet as shown on the left, or it can be eye spliced and served to make a tail block. The rope tail block is cheaper than modern equivalents with snap fittings; moreover it can be secured just about anywhere.

However for something more traditional why not buy the plain elm wood shells (from Thomas Foulkes Ltd) and put on the rope strop yourself? Apart from being very cheap the old rope-stropped block has much to commend it. It's lightweight and has no exposed metal parts to corrode, there is nothing to foul or snarl the sheets, there is a comfortable rope to cushion the bumps and, provided the sheave receives a good application of water-pump grease, it is practically silent in service.

Traditionally tarred hemp was used for the strop but prestretched terylene has even better non-rot properties. You need a piece long enough to go around the circumference of the block and thimble three times, plus just a little bit extra. The size of rope should correspond to the score in the block's cheek.

To make the strop, begin with a single strand of the rope and make it into a large overhand knot. Continue then laying up the rope into its natural pattern taking care not to disturb its inherent twist. Finish off with an overhand knot, then cut away half the yarns within each strand and tuck the remainder into the lay.

Figure 5

The shell requires several coats of varnish for protection, while prior to this a good soaking in linseed oil is similarly recommended. A simple round seizing is applied around the throat and this should squeeze the strop bar tight. In fact it's rather important that the strop is tight because this stops the pin coming out.

Blocks, iron-bound   They used to be called iron-bound blocks but the iron is now replaced with stainless steel. You can make these blocks yourself and to almost any shape or style you require. The block in the diagram (Figure 6) is a single sheave block but double blocks can be made equally well. Use hardwood, stainless steel straps and either nylon or bronze pulley wheels which you could get from a large hardware supplier or a fittings manufacturer.

Boat covers   Go to the firms which supply road transport tarpaulins for your boat cover and such sundry items. Huge volume production enable them to produce and sell much cheaper than sailmakers.

22

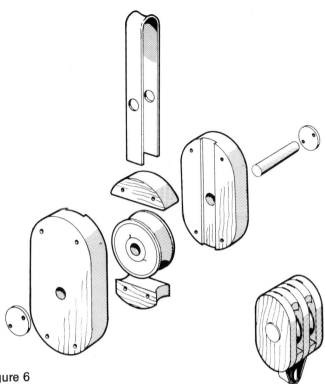

Figure 6

Boat World   This is boating industry's annual trade directory and contains the names and addresses of every manufacturer both in alphabetical order and also in separate lists under products. The particular advantage of this arrangement is that the reader can see at a glance the names of the manufacturers who supply, say, wind-driven generators or kit-built dinghies and write to them all for quotes. *Boat World* is on sale as a publication but – and here I'm ratting I'm afraid – your local library will hold a copy.

Building in composite wood and steel   One simple way to build the hull, decks and superstructure is a combination of 'chine' boat and ferro-cement technology. This is how the Marine View Boatbuilding Company of Tacoma, Washington, USA, builds boats; it claims it has reduced building time to a fraction, cut

23

down the amount of skilled labour time by 50 per cent and shown a remarkable saving in material costs.

Its system is to erect the framework with water pipe exactly as with a ferro-cement boat; the boat is given a hard chine configuration, instead of convex shapes, to facilitate laying the plywood which forms the skin. For the 54 ft (17 m) commercial fishing boats which the company produce, three skins of $\frac{1}{2}$ inch (12 mm) exterior building plywood is used. The first skin is fixed to the steel framework with ordinary pipe clamps and bolts while subsequent sheets are glued, nailed and bolted on where necessary. The decks and cabin structure are built the same way and for final protection the entire hull is sheathed with $\frac{1}{4}$ inch of reinforced epoxy resin.

Building in ferro-cement   The great economies in this construction are the materials and the fact that the hull can be built in the open. However, unless you have considerable experience I think it is a false economy to attempt the entire construction oneself as invariably a rather unlovely creation results (*see also* RESALE VALUE). It's better to buy a kit from somebody like MacAlister Carvall of Stem Lane, New Milton, Hants., or Ferro-Cement Marine Services of Ship Lane, Burnham, Essex. Apart from supplying the steel, wire and the correct cement, the kit includes ready-bent frames and a keel with slots cut at the stations. Contact with either of these firms will also provide professional advice and put you in touch with a team of experienced plasterers. If you are considering building in ferro-cement do your costings very carefully and compare them with other building mediums. Contrary to some claims it is not always the cheapest building method.

Building in GRP (glass reinforced plastic)   The customary manufacturer's kit including hull and deck mouldings, timber cut to size and main items of chandlery and equipment saves roughly 10 to 15 per cent of the completed price. It's a straightforward arrangement and little more needs to be said of it. However, to make a real killing you need to go much further back, to the bare mouldings at least and then follow the

24

recommendations made on the rest of these pages – or as many as ingenuity and integrity permit. But first of all how do you get a cheap set of mouldings?

Make a list of the GRP boats which you most admire and of a size that you think you could manage and then visit each of their factories. No matter whether the firm customarily sell mouldings or not, visit them anyway and put forward the following proposals:

1. Would they be prepared to hire their mould and some of their workmen on a Saturday morning so that you could have a hull built 'privately'?
2. Would they sell one of their old female moulds, if they have any, on the understanding that even under pain of torture you will never disclose where it came from – let alone ask for a sail number? You may have to recruit a building syndicate for this.
3. Would they be prepared to give you first option on the next hull that comes out damaged? Even the best builders have a 'stick-up' at some time and the knowledge that there is a ready buyer may persuade them that it is cheaper to sell than repair. (I knew a man, a sweet-talking man, who managed to acquire each one of the ten individual mouldings that went to make up a well-known motor sailer. All were damaged to some degree and all secured at a considerable reduction. What surprised us was not that a large company with a big production should have so many damaged items, but the way they seemed to turn up exactly when they were needed!)

Finally, if you don't have the neck to try any of these approaches simply ask what reduction they would give if you bought the mouldings and did all the filling and cleaning up that is necessary – they might get the message.

A recommended book for those who contemplate finishing a GRP hull is *Boat Building on a Glass Fibre Hull* by Dave Gannaway (Nautical Publishing Company).

Building in steel The price differential between steel and GRP continues to favour the former. Indeed while the pound falls and oil increases in price, the difference can only grow larger. So it is this consideration, plus the advent of modern epoxy paints, which inhibit rust so successfully, that have all helped to make the steel-built boat an extremely attractive proposition. Another traditional problem has been overcome: it is now possible to get a good unrippled shape without resorting to difficult framing. This is done by using chine or double chine construction, which obviates the need for plate bending. Several designs adapt themselves well to steel construction – the *Yachting Monthly* 'Eventide' or 'Goosander' are two examples – although some ready-built steel hulls are available.

John Teal suggests that the best way for the amateur to approach the job is to make a full-sized half model of the boat and then sheet this in hardboard. These hardboard sheets then become templates from which the actual plates can be cut by a sheet metal firm. Temporary frames (welded pipe is probably the easiest) are then erected upside down on a base and the steel sheets laid on to be welded. This method permits most of the welding both of the hull and interior to be done in one concentrated operation and saving a considerable amount in the hire of a welder or welding equipment.

If less than 30 feet the boat would almost certainly have a wooden deck and superstructure. One of the best books available on the subject is *Small Steel Craft* by Ian Nicholson (Adlard Coles).

Building in wood In the plain words of Howard L. Chapelle, one of the world's greatest authorities on wooden boatbuilding, 'a flat-bottomed boat is the least expensive' (when you're one of the world's leading authorities, you don't need to qualify your statements). To this we can add it is also the easiest and quickest. The archetype flat-bottomed boat is the Grand Banks' dory, renowned for her seakeeping qualities. There have been several sailing derivations and perhaps the most celebrated is *Erik the Red*, the boat John Ridler built in 1971 for £165 and sailed to and fro across the Atlantic.

Figure 7

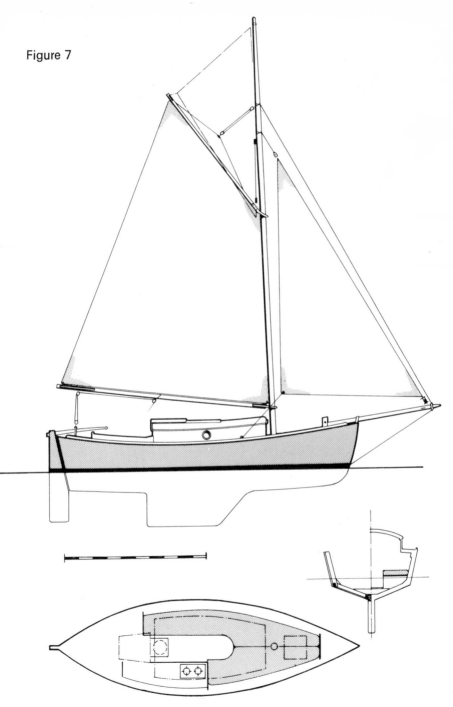

The other winning feature of the flat-bottomed boat is that in a good wind she is a remarkably fast sailer – *Mouette*, the boat upon which John Ridler based his design, is said to have made ten nautical miles downwind in just under the hour – and on several occasions!

The disadvantage of the dory type is that she is initially unstable and will need to be sailed more carefully. A further disadvantage is that with so little hull in the water the freeboard also must be kept correspondingly low, so there isn't too much room inside her. It is her tendency to be blown downwind which requires such a deep keel to compensate and in respect of a cheap mooring this may be seen as another disadvantage. In his book *Designing Small Craft* John Teal, who has built four flat-bottomed boats, shows how to design a 29-foot dory-type ketch with twin centreboards. With the plates up she has a draught of 8 inches (200 mm). (Imagine, no berthing fees, just leave her on the lawn overnight and float off with the morning dew.)

John Ridler's adventure was something too of a challenge to Des Sleightholme, the editor of *Yachting Monthly*. For some while he had been lamenting that it was no longer possible for hard-up young men to get afloat, the days of the 'tore-out' were gone, replaced by new and expensive technology. Consequently he had the original design redrawn, and just to show that the boat could be built cheaply and sailed safely, he commissioned one to be built. The design was called 'Mouette'; late in 1975 the first one was completed at a cost of just under £800. Mr Sleightholme sailed in this boat and his unbiased appraisal was published in *Yachting Monthly*, January 1976, p. 90. A set of six plans for 'Mouette' (alias *Erik the Red*) can be obtained by writing to Yachting Monthly Publications, Rochester, Kent, price £12.

Another genuine poor man's cruiser is 'Poppy', the design shown in Figure 7. She is a 22-footer designed by Paul Gartside of Bar Creek, Malpas, near Truro in Cornwall. Once again the dory influence is evident; although this boat has a vee bottom which gives her more headroom, more initial stability and reduces pounding – another of the flat-bottomed boat's small failings.

The designer says he drew her up as the cheapest possible cruising boat – cheap in terms of invested time and money. Naturally just how cheaply she can be built depends on the ingenuity of the builder in seeking out his fittings, etc., but the opportunity is there to build her for very little.

The hull is entirely straight-sectioned in order to make construction easy and, to simplify things still further, the bottom is cross-planked. Thus if the boat is built upside down, a lot of tricky building is avoided. The scantlings are large for a boat of her size; this again makes for economies such as the use of galvanized boat nails throughout the planking and decking, and the use of second-hand lumber. (John Ridler used old floorboards, although the large amount of recently felled elm now available quite cheaply makes elm seem a better proposition.) The boat is also shown with a gaff rig, although this is optional, and a ferro-cement keel, both of which, if built at home, can show a remarkable saving. (*See also* GAFF RIG *and* KEELS.)

Burglar alarm   Half the value of an alarm is that it should act as a deterrent which is why most manufacturers of car alarms supply window stickers. (And the thought occurs that you could have a burglar alarm 50 per cent efficient for the cost of one of these!) A home-made burglar alarm is simple to contrive, merely a case of running wires from the main and the fore-hatch to some device that makes a noise. This can be electrically fired, say, like a couple of Maserati air horns triggered off by the contact spring of a mouse trap. Or it can be manually operated such as a wire hooked directly on to the trigger of an aerosol horn. You will of course need to make them 'safe' from outside otherwise you'll scare yourself to death each time you go in.

Another cheap and effective arrangement is the 'body in bed'. This takes a little while to stage and some experience in amateur dramatics is of benefit. Stuff fenders and old clothes inside a sleeping bag and shape it so that it looks like a body, then put a wig protruding from the top. Also put a coffee cup and an open book by the side of the 'body' and a pair of trousers hung up on a hook. Finally leave a small night-light burning and pull the curtains back.

29

Buying direct   Such seems to be the high mark-up on chandlery items and equipment that it is worthwhile trying to buy from the factory direct. It may be necessary to buy in large quantities but this is where the group-buying facility of a club can have some effect. You will be pleasantly surprised just how many firms are prepared to sell direct and what a very businesslike service they give.

Savings to be made are obvious but to give you some idea here are two examples experienced. One home-builder of my acquaintance wanted some gunmetal coachbolts and his local chandler quoted a price of 80p each. However, he shopped around and finally discovered he could buy them direct from the factory in Birmingham, at a price of 20p each. Another yachting item he quoted is produced in a factory near his home and sold to the trade at 3p each. Incredibly, when this same item appears in the chandlery shops it is priced at £1·20.

Buying new   Unless you can find an ex-demonstration vessel at a well-reduced price there is no financial persuasion to buy from new, Value Added Tax has seen to that. The 'newest' boat you should consider is one about two years old. This is Hugh Marriott's advice who for many years ran a yacht brokerage business. Writing in his book *Owning a Boat* (Nautical Publishing Company) he says that a boat is past her initial depreciation period by the time she is two years old. What's more all the problems one associates with new boats will have been ironed out and wear will not yet be apparent. He suggests too that the best boat has belonged to a single, knowledgeable owner who has sailed her sensibly for two seasons – you might also hope that he is a wealthy man rather than a pauper and has crammed her full of nice, expensive gear.

Buying second-hand   There was a couple from Poole, who, in their search for a boat, scoured the whole of western Europe. Following various intelligence reports they went to Denmark, Holland, Ireland and Gibraltar. Finally, they found exactly what they wanted, in Lymington, not twenty miles away. It was a pity really; if they hadn't spent so much on travelling and telephone calls, it could have been a bargain.

If looking for a boat don't globe-trot – it's merely an extravagance. If you can't find something amongst the thousands of boats in, say, the Solent area you were probably not going to buy a boat anyway. Never follow up an advertisement for a far-off boat before first writing for full description and photographs. Search out the creeks and the down-at-heel yards and don't let appearances fool you. A mud-splattered, sad and neglected boat may be quite sound, and a survey could tell you. Look out for boats being sold by executors, boats that have been a long time on the market, and boats that have failed to sell at auction. Contact insurance companies. Sometimes a damaged craft which was under-insured is written off because high cost of labour makes repair uneconomical.

Then finally for a different tack try advertising in the 'Wanted' columns of the yachting magazines or *Exchange and Mart*. Quote the figure that you intend to spend. This has a strong persuasive effect, especially amongst those who hadn't considered selling their boats before the rates demand came in.

Cable   Adlard Coles once described how his boat was saved in a gale because a small grass anchor warp held firm after the chain cable had parted. He claimed that it was not the inherent strength of the rope but its elasticity and thus ability to absorb the enormous shock loads that had saved them.

That was in the 1920s. Since then we have seen the introduction of nylon which has even more stretch than coir and is probably six or seven times stronger. There is no doubt that nylon rope makes an excellent anchor warp and for our purposes it is much cheaper than chain cable. Moreover a nylon warp is easier to grip and very much lighter; you do not, for example, need an anchor winch which makes another considerable saving.

The objection to nylon warp, and this has to be mentioned, is that the boat does have a tendency to wander from side to side with each puff of wind. However, this can be minimized with the addition of 5 fathoms (10 m) of chain between anchor and warp to create resistance as it's dragged across the sea bed. The chain should be of near-compatible strength to the rope. Similarly an anchor weight or 'sentinel' suspended from the cable helps to make up for its lack of catenary or sag.

Car dump   Don't ignore the used-car dump as a good source for: parts of a twelve-volt system, such as fuel pumps converted for water galley supply, dynamos, bulbs, switches, and batteries sometimes; fuel tanks, gauges and piping; truck manifolds to make chain pipes; differentials to drive a trawl wire winch from the main shaft or converted to a hand-operated winch; Mini sub frames to make four-wheel boat trailers; Hardy-Spicer joints to take up the 'bend' in the tail shaft; horns; screen wipers; instruments; engine parts (even engines for conversion); and self-tapping screws by the dozen.

Chandlery   Unfortunately, the yacht retail trade seems to be under the delusion that the yachtsman is a man with money; whereas in the words of Mr Gerald Hammond who has provided quite a number of tips for this book, 'a yachtsman is someone who used to have money, before he bought a yacht'.

In consequence of this a great many chandlery items are priced far higher than they ought to be. On the other hand, farmers, fishermen and even the caravaners seem to be considered relatively impecunious because the self-same objects sold at any one of their retailers costs significantly less money. Here are a few samples I noted. One list gives quotations which are the average from three yacht chandleries. The other is a list of prices from an agricultural supplier situated not three miles away!

		Yacht chandler's	Agricultural supplier
Galvanized shackles	¼ inch (6 mm)	25p	18p
Galvanized shackles	⅜ inch (10 mm)	35p	30p
Bulldog grips	⅜ inch (10 mm)	24p	14p
Bulldog grips	⁵⁄₁₆ inch (8 mm)	19p	12p
Bottle screws (galvanized)	6 inch (150 mm) ×		
	⅜ inch (10 mm)	£1·97	£1·04

These are an indication of the savings that can be made on some identical items sold at both outlets. However, if you are prepared to accept the galvanized version then not only can you buy more of your chandlery at the agricultural shop but the saving is increased still more. The bottle screws quoted at £1·04 galvanized cost in stainless steel from a chandler's £5·33. Seizing wire, too. The popular way to sell seizing wire is in 'convenient' spools of 10-metre lengths. The wire is monel and it will cost you 60p. On the other hand if you are happy to use the old galvanized seizing wire then you can buy a 400-metre roll from the retail farm shop for £8·00, or about 20p for 10 metres.

A good source for other, more robust types of chandlery, plus oilskins and wire rope, is Cosalts Ltd, the fisherman's suppliers. They have fourteen branches around the country but if you are not within reach then they do operate a mail order service (address: Cosalts Ltd, Fish Dock Road, Grimsby).

It's a sad situation but a simple fact; if you want to save money in boating, avoid the swishy type of waterside chandlery shop. At least first consider whether the item you want might be bought cheaper elsewhere? Try caravan suppliers for gas stoves and gas fittings, twelve-volt electrical equipment, waste bins, storage jars, crockery, etc. Look into electrical wholesalers or engineering suppliers or even a used-car dump (see CAR DUMP). Remember too that large ironmongers sell small pulley blocks, brass fittings, oil lamps, sail twine and small stuff; that firms dealing with chain saws and motor mowers will probably have the spares for your outboard, while the dear old builder's merchant is an Aladdin's cave for plumber's fittings, paints, piping and stopping compounds. Put on your cloth cap and go round the back to the trade counter and you'll probably get things even cheaper.

Not only do you save money like this but if you ever cruise to a place where there is no chandler then such practised diversity could get you out of trouble.

Chart protection Charts which have to be used in the open can be waterproofed and given a much longer life if a layer of 'Transpaseal' or clear 'Fablon' adhesive is applied to the face side.

Chartering My feeling is that many of you, if I suggested that chartering was cheaper than owning, would see it not as an economy but a complete surrender. Owning a boat is fundamental to enjoyment and like you I believe that regular chartering is not to be contemplated.

I suspect, however, that the protagonists are right and that, measured in miles under the keel or even hours spent aboard, chartering works out cheaper. Still I don't care to look at their sums, not even to join in the argument which is against the whole spirit of the book. Most of us have no idea what our sailing costs and if we did we would cease to enjoy it.

Chartering your own boat Now this is more in line with what we are after. You will never make a lot of money but you should be able to offset your running costs – if you go about it properly. The thing is not to be too ambitious. In his book *Owning a Boat* (Nautical Publishing Company), Hugh Marriott, who was also connected with the charter business for many years, proved that a man with just one boat trying to charter full time in a typical English summer would find himself bankrupt by the second week in August. It simply does not work. By the time you have bought the right kind of boat, which he suggests should be a 26- to 28-foot twin keel, glass fibre, six-berth, cruising sloop with a diesel engine (although if the idea doesn't work I don't see why he bothers to tell us . . . ?), paid out for the inventory which must include liferaft, life-saving gear, bedding, crockery and cooking utensils, spare parts, etc., suffered the

34

heavy wear and tear on the gear, the additional depreciation, the marina berth, heavy insurance premium, advertising, postage, stationery, and printing, and then set this against the average charter rates he claims that it wouldn't even cover the annual costs, let alone the capital outlay.

It would be better to offer your boat to friends or people who are known to you; better still, since that arrangement can have its hazards and may well invalidate your insurance, work through your local charter company. Many of these are prepared to act as agents taking all the worry of finding bookings, etc., and subtracting a small percentage in commission. But satisfactory though this arrangement may be it's not very likely that your charter man will be happy to offer his clients an oakum-spewing gaff cutter with an engine that has to be fired with a blowlamp and a galvanized bucket for a toilet. You need the right kind of craft. And the right sort of gear also, otherwise it would be better to forget it.

This leaves us with the most sensible and profitable arrangement of all which is to skipper the boat yourself. It requires very little capital outlay, advertising can be done on works' notice-boards or parish magazines and what deficiencies there are (I'm thinking of that galvanized bucket) will quickly be submerged by your winning smile and engaging personality. In fact that is the trouble with this kind of chartering – you get so friendly with the crews it's a shame to take their money. Limit it to weekend trips, and to make them feel they are getting their money's worth, be sure to sail off on Friday night. A few miles down river to the pub should suffice. A friend of mine who charters like this claims to have enjoyed 'free' sailing for the past fifteen years.

Finally, if you do decide to charter in this way you may be able to come to some arrangement with your local sailing school in taking out parties of students. Motor boat owners of course can always take out fishermen.

Chronometer It's a case of modern technology overtaking traditional skills for there now is ample proof that the Smith's kitchen clock with battery and tuning fork movement is more accurate than the chronometer. A New Zealander who recently used this clock during a four-year world voyage claimed it gained at a constant rate of about two seconds a week, and that is much better than the average vessel's chronometer. Moreover he claimed it maintained the same accuracy in all weathers including a hurricane and stood up well to the biffs and bangs of shipboard life. He kept it safe in a biscuit tin.

Cleats Nothing shortens the life of a synthetic rope like chafe, and nothing produces chafe nearly so fast as a sharp-edged or an undersized cleat. Needless to say these are a common phenomenon these days. Moreover modern cleats are made of metal or hardened plastic which never gives the rope a chance to wear its own grooves or furrows. So the wooden cleat that you can make yourself is the best obtainable; it's large and it's 'soft' and it costs you virtually nothing.

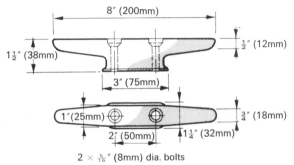

Figure 8

The cleats in the photograph are 8 inches (200 mm) long which are handy for most jobs on the boat; it is better to have too large than too small. They were made from a piece of oak picked up on the beach but any close-grained hardwood will do. Little skill is needed to fashion them. Simply draw the outline on to the wood and cut out the shape with a fine saw. Finish off with a rasp or surform tool and ten minutes' old-fashioned sandpapering.

It adds considerably to cleats' preservation to soak them in linseed oil.

36

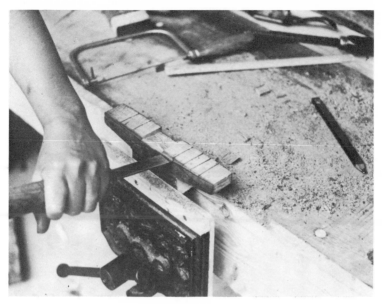

Transfer drawing on to the wood, saw and chisel roughly to shape.

Clean up with rasp and round 'Surform' tool, then sandpaper.

Clubs To suggest you join a yacht club simply because this saves you money would do more than devalue the spirit of the thing: it would also upset the members. Nonetheless membership of a club can reduce your boating bills considerably, providing you join the right kind of establishment. Think for a moment of the things that an energetic, influential and hopefully wealthy group of people should be able to achieve. Think of the skills and talents they have to call on. And all of it motivated by their love of boats and the only slightly subservient desire to save money. If your club isn't bursting at the seams with cost-saving projects and group-buying schemes, then get out and join another – or form one of your own! One like the Roa Island Boating Club for example. It was formed in 1963 as a limited liability company without share capital. Money was raised with interest-free loans from members – far cheaper than borrowing through a bank and it guarantees shareholders' continued enthusiasm! With this money and the members themselves doing most of the work, the club has been transformed from a wooden hut on the shore to an impressive and efficient establishment. (It includes such unheard-of things as a workshop with machine tools and welding equipment.) They have built a club-house, a starting-box, launching slips and roadways. They have also rebuilt a disused pier, repaired the embankments, erected scrubbing-off posts and hards, fixed up a winch, bought a crane and provided a club launching trolley. Each member provides his own launching trolley built to a standard design from a truck chassis and manufactured in the club's workshop. Lifting out is a communal activity and no charge is made; there is no charge either for electricity. Indeed the only costs involved are a mooring fee, a winter storage charge of £6·00 and an annual subscription of £8·50. All profits from the voluntary-run bar are ploughed back into the club as is money raised from various social activities. As the president, Mr W. Robertson, points out 'with schemes like this and a membership which includes every occupation from shipwright to solicitor we are pretty self-sufficient' – a sentiment also expressed by Mr Christopher Emmet who was the chairman of the Development Committee of Arun Yacht Club when they built themselves a

The Arun Yacht Club Marina nearing completion. DIY on a grand scale.

marina! The committee comprised an architect, an estate agent, a quantity surveyor, and an accountant: a complete range of skills for all the jobs available. However, he warns, any club considering a similar project should not underestimate the time and huge amount of work involved in the early stages of buying land, making the planning application and securing permission from harbour authorities and so on.

After the legalities had been settled, the costings suggested that pontoon moorings for sixty-six boats would equal about £20 000. Cruiser owners were invited to put up £250 in advance of mooring fees and this collectively raised about £11 000. The club already had £4000 and the bank agreed to meet the balance.

The depth of the excavation (which was done professionally) was determined by cost, which itself was governed by the cost of the disposal of the spoil. In the event they settled for a level at mean low water springs which meant that most boats could get in or out four hours either side of high water. The spoil was used to extend car and dinghy parks.

The piling and the welding of the pontoons was also professionally done but the deck and the placing of the polystyrene blocks were done by the members.

Regrettably inflation has overtaken estimates of running expenditure but nonetheless they expect to have paid off their overdraft within three years. By when the Arun Yacht Club will own a very considerable asset.

Collection   If you are building a boat then begin your collection of chandlery items and gear even before the keel is laid. Shopping over an extended period when things can be picked up at auctions or through advertisements is the only guaranteed way to economy. Imagine the rash expenditure there would be on the day of the launch if you suddenly found yourself without ropes or fenders, anchor or mooring warps.

Cooking   Two dark clouds loom over the cook who endeavours to cut down her food bill; one is that cooking afloat relies largely upon convenience foods which are expensive, and the other is that people in boats develop enormous appetites. There is nothing you can do about this but pray for rough weather or tie up alongside the city abattoir.

The dependence on convenience foods on the other hand can be reduced quite dramatically. I personally find it quite a relief to go a fortnight without a fiery plate of Madras curry or a packet of chicken kung-foo. Naturally you have to be sensible; it's quite ridiculous to lumber yourself with a hundredweight of King Edwards when the equivalent nourishment comes in a packet. (But I did know a man who carried a sackful of potatoes as trimming ballast – he reckoned it gave him an extra half knot on the wind!) Instant potato mixed with soups and stews increases their specific gravity, a very useful tip if you're catering in rough weather. Then again if you are going foreign it is only sensible to carry a large stock of dried and tinned foods because of the high cost of local provisions. Yet even so savings can be made by shopping wisely. Packet soups, for example, are cheaper than tinned soups, take up far less space and are usually much tastier. Dried milk too is cheaper than tinned milk and lasts indefinitely. Preservation of food is synonymous with economy and one should buy foodstuffs that will keep. Granary bread lasts almost indefinitely. Dutch cheeses too with their wax covering keep well. Breakfast cereals are not a good choice. Once opened they soon go soft; besides they take up an immense amount of storage space and see off an inordinate amount of milk – or rather the little people who demand them do. Far better to carry a bag of oats which can either be made into porridge or mixed with nuts, brown sugar and dried fruit and made into muesli. Either way you need very little milk and both are delightfully filling. Pasta, processed peas, lentils and beans are all good standbys and help to swell the stews and empty tummies. Tinned butter too is a good investment.

Naturally food lasts longer and tastes better if it is well wrapped and kept in such modern conveniences as aluminium foil, polythene bags and plastic boxes. Store bread in polythene bags and use foil to cover bacon, hams, cheese, sausages, etc. Eggs smeared with vaseline will last the ocean-going man for a considerable while.

If you have an ice-box then don't buy 'freezer packs': fill a plastic cordial container with water and freeze it. Placed in the ice-box this will keep butter, milk and beer cool for a weekend and provide ice-cold drinking water or even ice if needed. Also use the domestic freezer for preparing individually packaged meals, cakes, sandwiches, pre-cooked pies and vegetables. Home vegetables if previously blanched need little more than a toss in the frying pan before they are ready to serve. Stews are always popular. I sailed with a man whose contribution to the week's food was to bring some along in a jerrycan. It turned up again and again, re-heated and under a variety of pseudonyms: Irish stew, farmhouse stew, Lancashire hot pot, and when it finally became inedible he made it into a curry.

There is really no need for an oven. Joyce Sleightholme, who was for several years a cook with the Island Cruising Club, says in her book *The Seawife's Handbook* (Angus & Robertson) that the only advantage the 'oven' cook has over the person with a simple two-burner and grill is the facility of baking and keeping the plates warm. She suggests, as alternatives to roasting meat, grilling, braising in a frying pan, putting into stews or boiling. Toasted meals can be finished off under the grill which can also be used to warm up sausage rolls and small

Whatever happened to the plain delight of bacon frying on a primus stove? Not only are these utensils superfluous but just think of the chaos when she hits the first wave!

pies, provided an eye can be kept on them. Meat can also be cooked in aluminium foil if it is first seasoned, sealed tightly and then placed in water to boil. In fact the uses for aluminium foil are endless; warm up food by covering it with foil and then place it on top of an asbestos sheet on the burner (toast can also be made like this), or wrap separate items in foil when boiling them to prevent them and their flavours becoming mixed.

A pressure cooker is an obvious economy: not only does it save water, fuel and washing up, it meets that prime requirement aboard a boat of providing hot meals in a hurry. But if you don't want to invest in a pressure cooker or worry lest the little valve doesn't lift and your pie, mash and two veg. erupt and split the boat apart then at least get a good-quality saucepan and steamer. The saucepan is used for braising, stewing, frying or boiling while the steamer takes opened tins of different sorts to accompany the main course or pudding. Like the pressure cooker the combined saucepan and steamer only requires one burner. But in any event, whatever you use, frying pan, saucepan or whatever, make sure that all have good-fitting lids.

Two final economies. A spoonful of Bovril in hot water is cheaper than coffee with its sugar and milk; it's also quicker to serve, more nourishing and in most cases more warmly received. Carry a fishing line also.

Cove line   Use gold or coloured Scotch tape for the cove line and varnish for protection.

Craning out   Mobile crane operators charge at an hourly rate which commences from the time they leave to the time they return to base. If it is a half-hour journey and it takes only ten minutes to drop the boat in (or lift her out) then think how much money could be saved if there were two or three boats to lift in – or out! And particularly with all the owners on hand to help. If you propose to hire a crane announce the fact on the notice-board and tell everybody you can.

Crockery Cheap plastic ware is unattractive and unpleasant to use. The better grades cost nearly as much as china and are still unpleasant to use. Buy your boat's china crockery at the market stall.

Deadeyes The beauty of the old deadeye and lanyard method of staying the mast is that it permits a measure of flexibility to cushion the shocks and jars. As a result, in the days when they were commonplace, few boats ever lost their masts. Oddly enough the very point for which they were criticized – the need to adjust and preserve the rope falls – has now been corrected with the introduction of modern synthetic rope. For pre-stretched terylene remains stable, untroubled by rot and makes an infinitely stronger job.

    Deadeyes and lanyards are best suited to a heavy, broad-beamed boat where the high initial stabilty throws a more

Figure 9

immediate strain on the mast. Deadeyes can either be turned or carved from a block of hardwood as shown in Figure 9.

Deck preparation A good deck preparation for a wooden boat is first to cover the surface with molten pitch; spread this out evenly and allow it to harden, then lay on canvas and 'iron' it with an old flat iron. This will melt the pitch and cause it to soak into the fibres. Use aluminium paint to seal in the pitch and finally apply ordinary deck paint. This system gives a sound and waterproof cover which will last for years.

Deliveries For every owner who wants his boat moved, say from Lymington to Leeds, there will be somebody who wants a boat brought from Leeds to Lymington – owners are funny like that. And if you are considering having your boat transported by road then it is a good plan to contact the haulage firm well in advance of the date you plan and ask if they have anything booked in the opposite direction. If this can be arranged, and they are a reputable firm, you should secure a considerable reduction, and not only in the haulage rates, because, if the two operations are properly synchronized, you can save on craning charges as well.

Always get at least three quotations, especially when contemplating a sea delivery for these charges can vary enormously. (A few years ago quotations received to sail a fast yacht from the south coast to Sweden varied from £260 to £570.) Be very specific and ask whether the quotation includes the costs of the charts, fuel, extra insurance and the travelling expenses of the delivery crew. Such considerations may show that the quoted price was not as cheap as it appeared to be. Another point to establish at the outset is how much you will be charged if the boat is delayed due to mechanical or hull failure? This too can effect the price for the job considerably. Dismiss out of hand any firm which attempts to charge you for delays due to stress of weather; that's entirely their misfortune and a risk that should have been accounted for.

To reduce the cost of the crew's travelling expenses it is sensible to select a delivery firm based either at the place of departure or destination. For this reason too it is a good idea to ask the local boatyard who does their deliveries. Do as much as you can to ensure your boat is in a sound seaworthy condition before having her delivered. Ill-prepared boats are the bane of the delivery crew's existence and delays which occur while things are put right will inflate the price. Before you begin ask the delivery firm exactly what they need and what you can do to help them.

Explore all the possibilities; if your boat is small and slow then delivery by road will almost certainly be cheaper even though the overland distance is longer. Think too about delivery by canal and finally, as deck cargo aboard a ship. If the boat has her own cradle or can sit upright on her keels then deck cargo is undoubtedly the cheapest form of delivery. Amazingly, since the connection is close, few people ever seem to think of it!

Diesel   Fill up diesel (never petrol) tanks at the end of the season. Apart from giving you fuel at last year's price, it stops condensation in the tank.

Drip trays   An upturned drawer pull screwed or glued on the cabin side beneath a port glass makes the perfect drip tray to collect the droplets of condensation.

Elastic bands   Strips cut from tractor inner tubes make useful fastenings.

Exterior plywood (WPB – waterproof bonded)   It is a highly contentious point whether this material, which is less than half the price of marine ply, is suitable for boatbuilding. I have known of several people who have built boats, and pontoons, with various grades of exterior or shuttering plywood but despite satisfactory claims have never been able to inspect the results long afterwards. The principal differences between exterior and marine ply are in the quality of the timber, the number of laminations and the core thickness. Needless to say exterior ply is inferior in all these respects; the outside

46

veneer for example is paper thin (not so with birch or Douglas fir shuttering ply.) So, no matter how comparable the materials may be with regard to glue adhesion – and it is said that the same glue is used for both – there is a considerable deficiency in durability and strength, particularly impact strength. For this reason a heavier scantling of exterior ply will have to be used; if it is to be used for a hull or somewhere subject to continuous immersion, then it is probably necessary to sheath it with an epoxy resin preparation. Take these two considerations and I wonder whether there is much economy to be gained?

For wooden decks, coachroofs, interior furniture and places which you can easily inspect and protect then I would suggest that exterior plywood is acceptable – in any event it is what I have used.

Eyelets   Use a steel ball-bearing to hammer down eyelets, it will save you having to buy the punch.

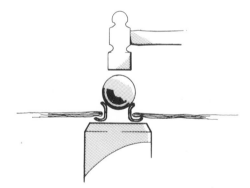

Figure 10

Fencing wire   Galvanized fencing wire, as sold by agricultural suppliers, has been used quite successfully for rigging small craft. It has a breaking strain well over half a ton.

Fenders and fendering   There is such an immense variety of improvised fendering materials that one wonders how manufacturers making the genuine item ever got a toe in the market. Take dinghy fendering for example; you can use coir rope or fire hose filled with foam granules, both of which need to be

Wire fence tensioners can be used for rigging screws.

wired on. Or you can use a run of split plastic garden hose fixed to the gunwale with self-tapping screws. If your boat is the type where the hull and deck mouldings meet together in a flange then a rubber hydraulic hose, suitably slit, can be slid over the flange. It is sufficiently resilient to hold without any fixing. Marleyrail is another alternative.

Single fenders can be made from Mini tyres (bandaged in canvas they look like a row of Polo mints). Hull Trinity House recently festooned their brand-new pilot launch with car tyres, claiming them to be the most practical form of fendering available! The old Board of Trade kapok life jackets chopped in half across the shoulders and fitted with eyelets will give you a pair of fenders. Or you can make the traditional fender from old lengths of rope half-hitched and stuffed full of rags. However, the half-hitching is a tedious business while the rope seems to shed more hairs round the boat than a Pyrenean mountain dog in a heatwave.

Figure 11 shows a cheap fender easily made from a short length of rope, a piece of sponge rubber and a square of canvas.

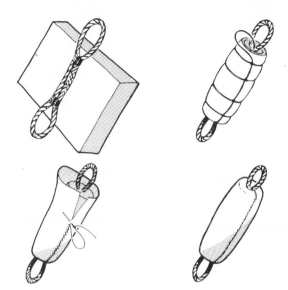

Figure 11

Before stitching on the canvas and tucking away the ends, wrap the sponge tightly in plastic to keep out the water.

Ferro-sheathing   Unless it is put on when the boat is new, glass fibre sheathing is rarely successful. In any event it's expensive. A far better method is to sheath an old wooden boat in ferrocement. Many boats have been saved from the graveyard with this method. Indeed the curious thing is that a large boat (and it needs to be a fairly large boat to be done successfully) will probably float higher in the water with a ferro shell than beforehand. This is because the heavy weight of water within the timber will have evaporated. For details contact a firm which specializes in ferro-cement construction.

Ferrule, D I Y   An improvised ferrule can be made by sliding a length of tubing over the two parts of wire, heating it up and filling the recess with solder. Ensure metals are compatible; do not use copper tubing with galvanized wire, etc.

Fiddles   The galley-stove kind: uncovered net curtain wires with cup hooks screwed in their ends are useful for restraining pots and pans.

Fillers It has been said that the only difference between new fillers and the old is that the packaging has been improved – a criticism which has to be left unproved since there aren't many of the old fillers left around to compare. Take Dr Worth's highly acclaimed wood filler for example (this is the man of the chain pawl acclaim, nothing to do with waggon stalls and hurried departures). It calls for beeswax, linseed oil, resin and genuine turpentine; by the time one has hunted that lot down and boiled it all together it would work out dearer than a drum of epoxy filler. In any event modern fillers are more convenient. They are cleaner, much easier to prepare and harden very much quicker – sometimes in the tin! They are also expensive. So here are a few cheap alternatives.

A resin glass putty can be made up by mixing ordinary lay-up resin with talcum powder or French chalk. When ready to use add catalyst, although rather more than usual.

Scratches and blister holes in the surface of a GRP boat are filled simply with a small quantity of gel coat resin and catalyst; if your local boatbuilder will let you scrape resin from the rim of the drum where it has thickened then so much the better. Use Sellotape to hold the mixture in place. Afterwards rub down with 'wet and dry' and polish with Brasso.

The time-honoured way to fill cracks in wood is with a mixture of sawdust and glue. However if the work is to be painted then quite good results have been claimed with Exterior Polyfilla. Dents in steel hulls can be filled with Portland cement mixed with 5 per cent washing soda. A mixture of cement and linseed oil makes a cheap filler for the seams of a wooden deck. It is easy to put in, clean and any excess can be wiped away at the time of application. It sets hard, no amount of heat can soften it and it is said to last for years. One disadvantage however is that it takes two or three days to dry.

Linseed oil putty still remains one of the best preparations of its kind; a good quality applied properly and left for a period will need a hammer and cold chisel to remove it (or nitric or hydrochloric acid applied with a brush). For mahogany-coloured putty try a greenhouse or cedar wood building supplier. Buy other filler preparations from a builder's merchant.

50

Filters   Fuel and air filters for the engine should be cleaned and replaced regularly. A blocked or dirty filter can increase fuel consumption quite significantly.

Fouling   Weed or marine growth on a boat's bottom causes drag which in turn means more power is required for the same speed – and that means increased fuel costs. Keep your boat's underside clean. A skin diver with a scrubbing brush sometimes comes cheaper than having the boat slipped at a yard.

Friends and neighbours   If you are building a boat announce the fact to as many of them as possible (and preferably with a hopeful smile, not by unsuppressed drilling coming through on their television). You will be delightfully surprised just what they can come up with.

Frost a window   Such is the variety of your sailing surroundings that the view from the toilet window can change in a moment from ocean blue to the inward gaze of a curious holiday-maker. You may be able to breathe on the window, or from where you are sat you may not be able to reach it; better to have something

The simple man with the simple boat can show us the real things in life; taking time out to manicure his fingernails.

permanent. Either a fine adhesive tint such as Letraset which can be bought from large stationers or a solution of Epsom salts and beer mixed together in the ratio 2 oz (50 g) Epsom salts to a cupful of beer. Stir until thoroughly dissolved and apply to the glass with a soft cloth. When dry give it a coat of clear varnish.

Fuel economy   A reduction in speed under engine is certain to reduce fuel consumption. It may take longer to reach your destination but you can console yourself: if your total time at sea is increasing at least the cost per hour is coming down. Generally the most economical speed is when the throttle is opened two-thirds, at least in the case of displacement boats. The first few knots are relatively cheap to attain but the cost rises steeply with the increase in speed. A thirty-five h.p. engine may be sufficient to drive a moderate sized boat along at seven knots but to gain an extra two knots an engine with double that power may be required. The editor of *Motor Boat and Yachting* suggests that to assess your boat's own most economical speed (without the expense of installing flowmeters) you must make repeated runs with varying throttle positions over a set distance. The average fuel gauge is not nearly accurate enough and consumption must be measured by the amount of fuel which later has to be put in the tank. Tide allowance will have to be taken into consideration, unless tests can be made in slack water.

Furniture   The drawers from an old mahogany or oak chest of drawers can usually be adapted to fit somewhere in a boat, under the bunks for instance. For lockers use sliding panels made from plywood offcuts fitted into plastic channelling obtainable from DIY shops. Handles for sliding lockers are an unnecessary expense and awkward protrusion; simply bore large diameter finger holes (they'll assist with the ventilation). The popular 'knotty pine' matching can be put to attractive use in the boat's interior. Moreover it is easier to fit neatly around the awkward curves and was, after all, the conventional cabin lining at one time. Use 'knotting' to cover the knots and

52

paint white or cream; in fact keep most of the interior light in colour, using mahogany trim for relief and decoration.

Gaff rig When all the arguments for and against gaff rig have died down there remains one clear and beautiful advantage, you can make it all yourself! A mast from the Forestry Commission's trees, mast hoops from riveted hickory, jaws from grown oak, gaff and boom from wooden scaffold poles and all the metal bits welded by your friendly garage man. Absolutely no concession given to weight and windage of course. Place those huge chunky fittings in the modern boutique-type chandlery and the 'easy-fit' shelving would come crumbling down. Figure 12 illustrates ways in which fittings can be made. The ideas, although traditional, are taken from the *Yachting Monthly* sponsored design 'Mouette'.

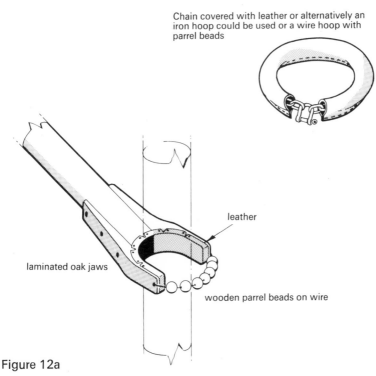

Chain covered with leather or alternatively an iron hoop could be used or a wire hoop with parrel beads

leather

laminated oak jaws

wooden parrel beads on wire

Figure 12a

Figure 12b

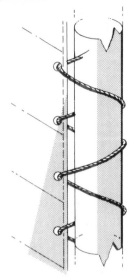
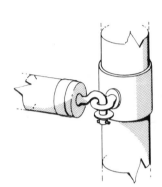

gooseneck arrangement

Luff simply laced to the mast (or home made
wooden mast hoops could be used)

Figure 12c

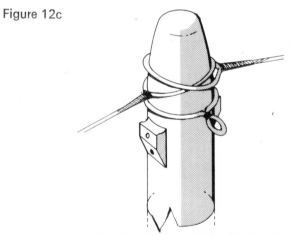

Shrouds and stays are simply spliced served,
varnished and slipped over the mast head
Oak cheeks secured to mast

Selvagee strop made from small galvanized wire rope and served

Figure 12d

Alternative mast band made from $\frac{1}{4}$" mild steel and galvanized

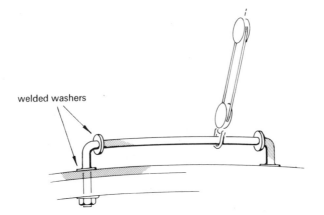

welded washers

Mainsheet horse made from $\frac{3}{4}$" mild steel bar

Galvanizing Many of the deck fittings which shine so temptingly in the chandlery shop window fail to measure up to the job. Either they have a nasty sharp edge, or a circumference too small for the rope intended, or they are not strong enough; also they are expensive. The small-budget buyer designs his own fitting, of generous section and massive strength, and then gets his local garage or blacksmith to make it. Then, when he has finally collected sufficient of these fittings to avoid the small-order surcharge, he takes them along to his local plant and has the whole lot galvanized.

Galvanizing gives a rough, rusty hunk of metal a beauty all its own, a functional, cart-horse beauty, the kind one associates with strength. It also keeps out the wet.

The small-order surcharge is usually based on weight although some firms simply make a minimum charge. Royal Naval dockyards undertake commercial galvanizing at competitive rates. Enquire before you begin.

Galvanizing (Chinese) This method of protective coating, actually used by the Chinese, is very effective. The fitting is heated to a cherry red glow and then plunged into a bucket of tar. (Mandarins once did the same with mutinous peasants.) If the tar catches fire quench immediately with a cupful of water. The tar is baked on and adheres with greater determination.

Galvanizing rigging wire There is an old master rigger in Poole who tells the story of how he used the same set of galvanized plough laid rigging in the same yacht for twenty-five years! At the end of each season he stripped the mast and over the winter soaked the wire in a bath of boiled linseed oil. He did this religiously every year until the yacht was finally sold. The new owner was an American (I'm not clear how nationality effects the story but the old chap was quite emphatic) and the American decided that as the rigging was now over twenty years old he ought to have it renewed. He ordered a set of new stainless steel rigging which, the rigger claimed, cost four times as much as the galvanized one.

Nine months later when the yacht was surveyed it was found that the stainless steel wire had fractured and had to be condemned. So, cap in hand, the American owner went back to the rigger who gleefully fished the old galvanized wire out of his bath and with immense satisfaction put it back on the yacht.

Now our master rigger is dreadfully biased (he also condemns the modern practice of using flexible, or PVC-covered wire for guardrails in preference to the old plough laid galvanized stuff), then again it is possible that this particular batch of stainless steel wire was below standard. Still we're not arguing the merits of one against the other, simply trying to show that the cheaper galvanized wire, properly looked after, is more than good enough.

(If you wish to dress rigging without stripping the mast try this tip: wrap a sponge well soaked in boiled linseed oil tightly around the shroud or stay and to prevent drips on the deck, cover this with a piece of polythene. Bind this well, hook on to a convenient halyard and hoist slowly aloft. Mix varnish with the boiled oil for fast drying.)

Gas detector   Pumping the bilge dry directly you step aboard and giving a few extra strokes after discharge has finished clears the bilge of any errant gas and the need for a gas detector instrument.

Genoa track and sliding fittings   A cheap alternative to a genoa track and slide is to fit galvanized eyebolts through the deck at intervals of 9 inches (250 mm). The sheet lead can be switched quite quickly to whichever eyebolt is required by the expedient use of a snap shackle. The lead bolt is held vertical by a length of shock cord hooked to the guardrails. Owners who have adopted this idea claim it is as efficient as the deck track and has an added advantage, for the eyebolts provide useful fixing points for various other operations.

On the other hand you can make do with just one fixed jib sheet lead if each sail has its own set length of tack wire (Figure 13). (*See also* TACK DOWNHAUL.)

Figure 13

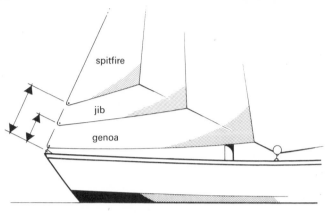

Tack wires of different lengths allow one
fairlead to be used for all head sails

Glass fibre mat   The scraps of glass mat that boatbuilders throw away will more than cover the requirements of most little jobs on the boat. Jobs such as repairs, stiffening, and bonding in items of furniture require only very small segments of mat, in fact just about the size that you find in the boatbuilder's dustbin.

Guardrail lashings   Instead of securing guardrails with those small nylon connectors (which have been known to fail) it is far safer, cheaper and more seamanlike to use terylene lashings at each end. They are simple to rig, easy to let go and in cases of emergency can be cut through with a knife. To ensure they are set up tight, use the method shown in Figure 14 which provides a small purchase.

Figure 14

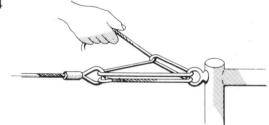

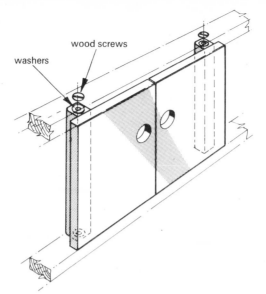

washers

wood screws

Figure 15

Hinges It is difficult to find brass hinges with anything but a steel pin which of course will rust. One way out is to make hinges from hardwood or plywood (Figure 15). Ordinary sliding door bolts make excellent removable hinges.

Houseboats It is still possible to live permanently aboard a boat however much local councils may do to dissuade you. The point is that you must select a proper sea-going job and reject any you are shown with window boxes and chimney pots. The last thing that any official wants to see is one of these steaming round the breakwater looking for a last resting place.

But if you are prepared to sacrifice a little space (and confined conditions are something you adjust to) then, quite apart from the fun, living aboard a boat does offer distinct financial advantages. It is cheaper than buying a house, you qualify for a marine mortgage with the usual tax concessions and you almost certainly will not have to pay rates – or if you do you simply move on again.

In fact being able to move on, or at least being prepared to, is the prime requirement. Very few marinas and harbours object to you living permanently aboard if they can get rid of you if they have to. So don't let the problem of finding a mooring put you off. Simply present yourself at the place of your choice and tell them you would like to stay for a couple of days. And then, if you're well behaved, the days turn to weeks and the weeks turn to months and before you know it they won't have the heart to ask you to move. Alternatively if you are not the lovable kind then you must try to make yourself indispensable.

And you needn't confine yourself to a harbour with all the hustle and bustle to disturb you. Why not instead try the rivers and canals and the delights of the English countryside? I heard of a man who did this for years, keeping his boat on the canals and moving on every two months or so. He was still able to commute to his job in the City and to all outward appearances might have owned a villa in Surbiton. The prime requirement here is not so much the boat but a good memory.

It doesn't have to be the typical boxy canal boat. A flat-bottomed ketch such as John Teal has designed (*see* BUILDING IN WOOD) or an Ocean Bird type of trimaran with sponsons on hinges which tuck into the side of the main hull means your boat is narrow and shallow enough to sail the canals while remaining a real, sea-going craft.

Insurance You can sail without insurance; some people do. The Arab dhow sailors for example; they believe it wrong to make provision for what they see as the will of Allah. In short, to them insurance is sinful. Probably this accounts for a certain amount of backsliding and no doubt poor Allah gets blamed for more than he would normally cause. But nevertheless one has to admire their readiness to take life on the chin, which is more than many of us seem prepared to do.

Still there is a world of difference between the Shatt al Arab and the river Hamble where an uninsured yacht, eloping with its chain, can easily inflict many thousands of pounds worth of damage on its neighbours. It would be hard for the owner of that unfortunate vessel to see it as just another knock on the chin. Perhaps if we were the most meticulous and experienced seamen and lived aboard our boats continuously, we might get away without insurance. But most of the time our boats are left unattended on a berth or on a mooring and this is when most of the trouble occurs, in harbours and marinas. Nobody today can sensibly go without third party insurance – Arab or infidel.

It isn't strictly accurate to speak of comprehensive policies with marine insurance but we can stick with the term for the moment. Do you need a comprehensive policy? One well-established insurance broker I spoke to put it this way: most people would be distressed if they lost their boat and even financially embarrassed, but very few would find their entire lives ruined – very few except those who live aboard or use their boat for their livelihood would find themselves bankrupt. Therefore you should look at insurance in this context – can you afford the loss of the boat? And if the answer is 'yes', then you must compare the premium asked against the eventuality of the boat's loss. If the answer is 'no' then you must insure.

The word 'comprehensive' or 'all risks' to describe a policy is bandied about far too easily by some insurance agents and brokers. 'Comprehensive' really means a policy of 'specifically stated perils' which does not cover every manner of marine disaster by any means, *only those which are stated in the policy*. A genuine all risks policy, on the other hand, covers *every risk other than those exceptions actually stated in the policy*. It sounds a little confusing but you can understand there is an enormous difference. And it is important to nail your broker, agent or whoever you deal with and not be fooled by glib references.

Make sure you get the best cover for what you have to pay; this is the real economy. Go to a large and established firm of brokers rather than to a boatyard or local insurance agent. This is not disloyal, merely good sense. A broker is a full-time professional man and insurance is his business. On the other hand insurance to a boatyard or an agent may be just a sideline or a customer service. The broker has a much larger field to play; he can seek quotations from each of the established companies (including the one represented by the agent) and will know from experience which is the best to place your business with. Moreover, he will have access to Lloyd's underwriters who quite often offer the most competitive rates. Without the broker's specialized knowledge it is almost impossible for an outsider to tap this wide and valuable market. Do not believe that you can save money by dealing direct with an insurance company. It's true brokers can earn up to 15 per cent of the premium on all business introduced but for this they also do a great deal of work.

Ask your broker for two separate quotations; one which provides the best possible cover and the other giving the cheapest. Then decide for yourself.

Don't buy more insurance than you need. If you sail on a non-tidal lake or never cruise more than ten miles from your home then make sure your broker understands this. Do not pay for 'UK Coastal' or 'Continental' cover if you never go abroad; you can always request a temporary extension if you do. Similarly, if you never race your boat or loan it to other people, or do not carry expensive navigational equipment or personal effects, then savings here can also be made. Again if you inform your broker in advance that you are not going to use your boat one season you can obtain a quotation for laid-up risk and third party cover only, which should save between 30 and 40 per cent of the premium. If you are building a boat then ask for 'building risk' cover which works on a sliding scale geared to the boat's increasing value; it's cheaper than full cover.

You can also reduce your premiums considerably if you are prepared to accept a large excess, or in other words pay a proportion of any damage. For example, the gross annual premium for a £10000 yacht before no claims bonus is approximately £125. A £50 excess saves approximately £15 on the premium whereas a £100 excess saves approximately £35 – a quite considerable saving. But before you undertake a heavy 'excess', consider the effect of two claims one shortly after the other. Could you afford the double excess?

Certain policies provide additional discounts if the boat is left in a harbour or marina which is considered safe and protected, or if the owner has a yachtmaster's certificate or fits certain safety features to the boat. Then again certain class associations to which you may belong secure reductions by buying insurance in bulk, although these arrangements are not always cheaper for all types of boats. In any event shop around if only for the exercise; you could be paying a higher premium than you need.

Jib sheet fastening   A snap shackle used for a jib sheet fastening is a calamitous idea. When it's not clattering against the mast like a demented woodpecker it's trying to smash your glasses or knock our your teeth – and there is a double indignity in getting hit by a fitting that you paid so much money for! Instead

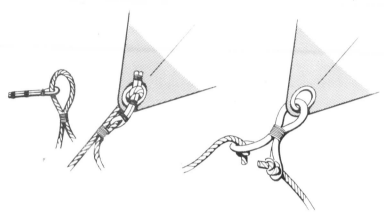

Figure 16

try this rope eye and toggle arrangement; you get a much softer blow for nothing. It will hold secure in all conditions even when the boat is head to wind with the sails shaking wildly.

Keels   Steel for centre plates or bilge keels can nearly always be bought from a scrapyard. Provided you supply a hardboard template the local garage man or blacksmith can do the cutting and welding.

Keels, ferro-cement   Ferro-cement is probably the simplest and most effective material with which to build a fin or a bilge keel. There is no expensive steel plate to buy and no cutting equipment needed. The wire mesh and rods are simply laid over a rough wooden mould and the mortar is plastered on.

63

Other advantages are that a ferro keel can be aerodynamically shaped and that the weights – pig iron, lead or whatever – can be loaded into the centre. This way they are held solidly in place and their weight is pitched low down. A ferro keel can be fixed to almost any hull material. In wooden boats this obviates the need for a deadwood.

A one-time Admiral's Cup boat *Mersea Oyster* was given a ferro-cement keel. It was done to improve her windward performance, not as an economy.

Keels, twin   There is no doubt that a twin keel (or centreboard) boat does show a saving. It provides the facility of self-launching from a trailer and storing at home, and it also means that the boat can be left on a half-tide mooring, almost invariably cheaper than one in deep water. Moreover a twin keel boat can be beached for the night or left to dry out in some creek while its deep keel sister will have to lie in a marina. Laid up ashore she doesn't require to be chocked off nor does she ever need a cradle, so that handling charges should be cheaper. Finally a shallow draught boat may enable you to moor in a river or creek near to your home thus saving a considerable amount of car mileage.

Kits   You can buy kits for just about everything: kits to build boats, to make radios, trailers, self-steering gear, kits to marinize engines. The increased levy of VAT gave a huge boost to kit-building and caused many suppliers to either initiate or improve existing arrangements. (During the twelve-month period when VAT was at the luxury rate of 25 per cent one company, Marcon Yachts, were selling 95 per cent of their boats on the home market in a kit form of some sort!) You still have to pay VAT on the parts of course, but not on your labour. So there is this saving which is over and above all previous considerations. Before buying anything check to see if it is available in kit form; the trade reference *Boat World* will usually tell you.

Leadline Any lubberly type can switch on an echo-sounder but it takes a seaman's skill to use a leadline (a sentiment you would readily concede had you been on my training cruise and seen one lad twirl it around the yardarm and another fire it down the fore-hatch). What's more the hand-lead gives you far better accuracy in those shallow, keel-scraping depths. Then again if you take the trouble to 'arm' the lead with tallow or soap you can find out the type of sea bed – useful when taking the ground and something you can't do with an echo-sounder.

A lead is easily made at home. For a 3 lb ($1\frac{1}{2}$ kg) lead, which is adequate for most shallow depths, you will need to collect about $3\frac{3}{4}$lb (2 kg) of scrap lead. (I don't for the life of me know where the extra $\frac{3}{4}$ lb goes.) This can be made up from plumber's pipe, lead cable, flashing, car battery plates or toy soldiers or farm animals. Melt them down in an aluminium saucepan or a large tin suitably squeezed into a spout shape for pouring. Molten lead can be dangerous so be careful; either wear glasses and adequate clothing or fix up your tin with a long wooden handle so that you never need to be in close contact. Be warned too against using a receptacle with soldered joints, while to preserve marital harmony do the smelting on a camping stove away from the kitchen.

left The melting pot, the wooden mould and the sand tray.

right The completed lead filed and cleaned up with 'Surform' tool and ready for line. (This same item in a chandlery shop was priced at £3.)

You need a sand tray to stand the mould in and a quantity of damp sand. It must be damp, not wet for this will cause a violent reaction on contact with the molten lead. The mould can be made from plywood. It is four-sided and should be 6 inches (150 mm) high and measure $1\frac{1}{4}$ inches (32 mm) square at base and $\frac{3}{4}$ inches (18 mm) square at the top. Make the joint edges as clean as you can and just to be sure they don't leak bind the mould tightly with aluminium foil. Place a pebble in the sand for the indentation at the bottom of the lead and place the mould centrally over it.

Pour the lead slowly and allow to cool thoroughly before attempting to break open the mould. The lead of course has a very rough appearance at first but this is soon cleaned up with a file. Hammer the top flat and drill a hole to take the leather becket or shackle.

The line can be as long or as short as you wish, depending on the area you cruise in. Similarly the markings can be to your own choice; there is no compulsion to stick with the traditional.

Swinging the lead you'll find is a very satisfying occupation but do remember to make the inboard end secure before casting. The third novice, I seem to remember, forgot this and ended the exercise prematurely. Still, the way things were going that was probably our good fortune.

Leaks Leaks ought to be like accidents that can happen to anyone, but it rarely turns out that way. The poor with their ailing wooden boats have a built-in predisposition. Perhaps this is why there aren't any expensive leak-stoppers on the market? The rich don't want them and the poor can't afford them! And if there aren't any *expensive* leak-stoppers then we can't suggest any cheap alternatives. . . . Here are the old ones anyway.

Seams of a wooden boat can be plugged with yellow soap. On contact with sea water the soap first softens and then solidifies to take on the consistency of processed cheese. Indeed yellow soap was the standard caulking compound in the old Cornish luggers which were planked with softwood on oak. Unfortunately it only works in sea water; somebody once took a lugger up the Thames and somewhere above Teddington she lathered up and sank.

Another standard practice was to plug temporarily the seams of a wooden boat with sawdust. In the days of the old 'coffin' ships on the Baltic timber trade there was always great competition to load nearest the mill where the sawdust in the water would enter the seams and then, as the vessel was loaded to her marks, be pressed in and held under pressure. The French ocean voyager Bernard Moitessier suggests that the best remedy for leaking garboards is to dive overboard with a tin of sawdust. Keep the tin inverted until beneath the leak when it should be turned to let the contents float out and find its way into the seam.

In G R P boats the difficulty is getting anything to stick to the gel coat when it is wet, although if you can dry the surface then duct tape, which is used by sheet-metal workers to seal joints in duct-work, is said to be very effective. In the main, leaks in G R P boats have to be temporarily plugged from the inside, in which case the solutions for wooden boats might apply. These include cement boxes – merely a rough wooden box built around the area where the leak is situated and filled with cement; a good fistful of butter, soft soap or grease slapped over the leak, or a mixture that was commonly used by fishermen on the north-east coast which comprised sawdust, tar and horse dung. Difficult though to persuade the horse of the urgency.

Lifeboat conversions Converting a lifeboat has always been the popular way for the poor man to get afloat although perhaps now with the availability of G R P hulls for home completion the fashion has waned a little. And yet I'm not so sure that it still isn't the cheapest method; at the end of 1976 the P & O company sold off a number of 26- and 30-foot G R P lifeboats fitted with diesel engines and all said to be in good condition for £1300 each!

The Ministry of Defence are another good source and sell anything from small gunboats to sailing dinghies. These are sold by tender at various establishments around the country where you are able to view them by arrangement. Your bids

Ex-ships' lifeboats in Belsize yard in Southampton.

must be sent in writing to the Director of Navy Contracts (Ships), Room 105, Block F, Foxhill, Bath. An application to this address will also secure a list of craft currently up for disposal. Other addresses to which to write to for ship's lifeboats are: P & O Lines, Peel Street, Northam, Southampton; Belsize Boatyard, Priory Road, St Denys, Southampton; Dolphin Engineering Co., Old Leigh High Street, Leigh-on-Sea, Essex. A good book to buy is *Lifeboat into Yacht*, price 25p from Yachting Monthly Publications, Rochester, Kent.

Liferafts Liferafts, along with a whole range of other expensive equipment, can be hired rather than purchased. And if they are only required for peace of mind during the summer cruise then hiring is an obvious attraction. Borogear Ltd, of Tiptree, Essex are long established in the liferaft hire field. The gear can either be collected or despatched by van or passenger train.

Lining Use ordinary hessian to line the inside of a GRP boat: it looks so much more ship-shape than quilted foams. These are fine for brothels and padded cells but look terrible in boats. If the hull surface has been left bare then the hessian can be 'glued' on with a generous application of lay-up resin. A good soaking of this will help the material to stiffen the hull; indeed at one time some builders included a layer of hessian or jute in their hull and deck laminations. Alternatively, the material can be stuck on with ordinary rubber adhesive. When dry, paint with emulsion. Hessian can be bought in a selection of weights and weaves from upholstery shops.

Another idea is to bond wooden fillets to the hull and then screw mahogany or softwood slats to them. Secured in the fore and aft line they look very attractive and if placed alongside bunks allow a good air flow and prevent sleeping bags coming into contact with the moisture on the hull.

Log There is abolutely no need for you to spend your money on a log line. If it's the boat's speed you want or the distance run then here are a selection of methods that have been used successfully down through the ages. (Unfortunately most of these ideas are pretty labour-intensive; still they should keep children and charter crews out of mischief.) The Dutchman's log, for example, will delight you with its rustic simplicity for it requires no more than a piece of wood and the attentions of three grown men.

Dutchman's log. One man stands in the bows and heaves a piece of wood ahead of the boat – not too near so that it is disturbed by the boat's bow wave as it passes, and not too far out so that nobody can see it. He sings out the exact moment the stem passes it. A second man, stood in the stern, sings out the exact moment the stern passes it, while a third man times the process. Now here comes one of those very rare occasions where metrication makes things easy (at least for the over-thirties) because if you express the length of the boat in metres, double it, and then divide this figure by the number of seconds counted you end up with a number which is actually the speed of the boat in *knots*!

The arithmetic of this is based on the fact that one sea mile is near enough 1800 metres and that one hour is 3600 seconds; hence:

$$\frac{\text{metres} \times 2}{\text{seconds}} = \text{knots}$$

For greater accuracy do the whole thing a few times over.

Log chip. The term 'knot' derives from the days when, to estimate speed, a line was thrown over the stern and timed as it ran out. The line was marked in lengths and each were proportionate to the nautical mile as the period of the sand glass was proportionate to the hour. In other words, they were equivalent fractions. The lengths were marked with knots and all the operator had to do was to let the line run out through his hand and watch for the last grain of sand to drop. When this happened he would have the ship's speed – in *knots*.

You can make a hand log yourself quite simply. The one shown here in Figure 17 was designed by a Master Mariner, Mr T. J. Williams, and first published in his book *Coastal Navigation*.

Figure 17

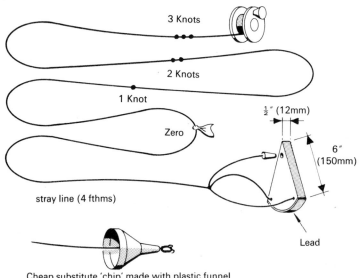

3 Knots

2 Knots

1 Knot

Zero

½" (12mm)

6"
(150mm)

stray line (4 fthms)

Lead

Cheap substitute 'chip' made with plastic funnel
and secured to shackle for weight

The log chip is a triangular-shaped piece of wood weighted with a piece of lead along its bottom and attached by a three-part bridle. The purpose of the bridle, one leg of which is secured to a wooden plug, is to make the chip sit upright in the water and create enough drag to remain stationary. To hand the log simply give the line a sharp tug to free the plug and the log chip will capsize. The line is thin braided terylene and to be sure that the chip is carried clear of the boat's wake, where the eddies would give a false reading, at least four fathoms called the 'stray line' is allowed to run out before the zero mark.

The line is divided into lengths of 25 feet 4 inches and each division marked with a knot. This measurement is exactly 1/240th part of a nautical mile which corresponds with a timing period of 15 seconds (which is 1/240th part of an hour). You can use a wristwatch.

With practice the log chip will give accurate results.

Something that will make the Walker Log people tremble in their boots is a design I am working on which incorporates the usual log rotator coupled up to a pram wheel and an old bicycle speedometer – I started with a car speedo but 120 m.p.h. seemed a bit optimistic. Sadly I hadn't perfected it by time this book went to press so please feel free to take up the idea; I shan't bother about patents.

Maintenance, engine An engine that craves attention will manifestly make more noise and burn more fuel. If the valves don't seat properly or the piston rings are worn then it cannot develop the power it should for the amount of fuel burned. Other areas which cause fuel wastage are the ignition and carburation system in a petrol engine, and fuel pump setting and calibration of a diesel's injectors.

Marine conversion, engine The cheapest engine for a boat is the marine conversion of an ordinary car or truck engine. The unit is basically the same except that it has a bell housing and marine gearbox, an oil pump fitted to the sump, a larger water pump, extra piping and a water-jacketed manifold. Although there are firms which undertake this conversion and then sell marinized engines under their own trade name, it is possible to buy conversion kits and do the job yourself (see *Boat World* for addresses). Some firms sell the factory-reconditioned unit but it is cheaper to pick up a good second-hand engine, preferably from an insurance company with a 'write-off' to sell (a scrapyard is the other alternative), and do the necessary overhaul. The Ford 100E is probably the cheapest and most popular of the petrol engines for conversion, while one of the Ford 4D range is a favoured diesel. If you really want the best advice in this field and a blow-by-blow account of how to do it then look at Nigel Warren's book *Marine Conversions* (Nautical Publishing Company) or at *The Complete Motor Yachtsman's Manual* by Loris Goring (Nautical Publishing Company), another very sound book on the subject of engines, and in fact all aspects of motorboat maintenance.

Marine mortgage Unfortunately the Government have scrapped the concession which allowed tax relief on the interest paid when buying a boat on a mortgage. There is, however, still a concession if you live on the boat and use it as a permanent residence. You can in this instance get tax relief on a loan either to buy or improve your floating home. And it needn't necessarily be a houseboat as such. The terminology used is 'boat or similar structure designed or adapted for use as a place of permanent habitation'.

Additionally, I have seen advertised the 'Mayflower Ten Year Marine Mortgage' in association with the Minster Insurance Company (other companies may operate something similar). This is a mortgage linked to an endowment life assurance policy where the applicant takes out a ten-year policy equal to the amount loaned. When the policy matures, this is used to pay off the advance. However, as a portion of the monthly payments goes towards the insurance premium income tax relief can be claimed in the usual manner.

In accordance with all marine mortgages, the boat must be registered, or registerable and in this case not more than five years old. The advance will not exceed 80 per cent of the value of the craft and the minimum advance is £1500. As an example

72

they quote a loan of £5000 over ten years. This works out at £99·98 per month including an annual income tax relief at 35p in the £ of £95·38.

Masonite This is an oil-tempered hardboard, about $\frac{3}{4}$ inches (18 mm) thick. It is a durable, waterproof material and comparatively cheap. It can be used for many jobs in the boat's interior, and is rigid and easy to work. Just how durable it is may be proved by the fact that many years ago Ben Carlin who sailed and motored around the world in an amphibious jeep used Masonite to build his cabin top. (You'll notice how we cheapskate builders have no difficulty whistling up names, and notice how frequently we do it.) By coincidence the garden shed in which I wrote this book is a timber-framed construction sheathed with Masonite. I am ashamed to say that apart from sealing the edges and butts I haven't got around to painting it yet. Nevertheless after two and a half years it is still perfectly sound – a little sunbleached perhaps. Curiously enough Masonite looks very attractive when varnished and might even be taken for bird's-eye walnut at a distance.

Masts, alloy Before buying a metal mast do write around for quotes; the prices vary considerably. There are a few metal mast manufacturers who will supply extrusions and fittings for home assembly and one such is Kemp Masts Limited, St Margaret's Lane, Titchfield, Hants. Anodizing can add more than £20 to the cost of a moderate-sized mast which can be saved if the mast is painted or varnished with a two-can preparation. Delivery charges can be eliminated altogether if the local cub or brownie pack can be persuaded to walk it home centipede fashion.

Masts, cannibalized It is surprising just how many small cruisers sport ex-dinghy or day-boat masts. Generally they are wooden masts discarded when the popular 'class' switched over to aluminium, or they may be an ex-keel boat's mast that has snapped – quite a number do in the hard-sailing championships. Next time bad weather threatens to *spoil* one of these events

73

why not be on hand with your cheque book? Those with foresight could make an obvious saving if they design their rigging plan so that the popular, ready-made dinghy or day-boat masts and sails can be employed; in this application a ketch rig is the most desirable. In all events you need to step the mast at deck level.

Masts, hollow wooden   A hollow wooden mast made yourself and complete with fittings should be about half the cost of factory-built masts made of alloy. The two most popular methods of construction are shown in Figure 18. It is a matter of

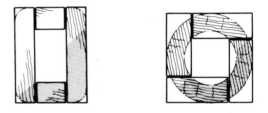

Figure 18

preference whether you leave the mast rectangular, but obviously rounding off and spindling out gains great saving in weight; indeed a 'rounded' mast need only be about 50 per cent heavier than one made in alloy. Douglas fir is a good substitute for sitka or spruce which is difficult to acquire these days. (Try someone who imports timber to build wooden ladders.) It is doubtful that you will be able to buy the wood in the complete length you require so scarphing will be necessary. Make sure that the wood you select is free from blemish and twist and has been thoroughly seasoned. The mast must be constructed on a dead-level surface which can either be got from a row of boxes or trestles; from T-stakes driven in the ground; or by the use of brackets screwed into a wall. The cramps, and you will need dozens of these, are made up from fence bolts and banister rods (Figure 19), or some such substitute materials. There is not space in this book to detail step-by-step construction but two very sound articles on the subject have already been published. One is to be found in *Yachting Monthly*, May 1972, page 730, and the other in *Practical Boatowner*, May 1970, page 58.

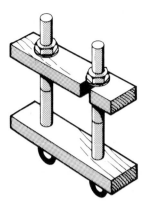

Figure 19

Masts, lattice (open-frame) These masts, which are as rigid as those made of wood or metal, have been made in Australia and America for several years and are claimed to be very successful. They are made from electrical conduit or water pipe. Individual designs vary but the general idea is to weld three lengths in the form of a triangle. The top and bottom of the mast is tapered and braced throughout its length by rungs welded at 15 inch (375 mm) centres. A mast track is attached with screws or pop rivets and all the halyards are 'internal'. It requires the usual staying arrangements.

Advantages of the lattice mast are that it is extremely simple and cheap to construct, and it is said to give a much better air flow on to the sail. The disadvantage is that it requires more maintenance; as climbing the mast is relatively easy this isn't too much of a misery. Besides the problem is largely overcome with galvanizing.

A British designer and champion of the amateur boatbuilder, John Teal, has included lattice masts in a 29-foot cruising ketch (Figure 20).

Mast, lowering and raising The current boatyard charge for stepping or unstepping a mast is about £8·50 (half as much again on Saturdays and double on Sundays). With a mast stepped in a tabernacle you could do this yourself for nothing. If you are lucky enough to berth near a low bridge or can lay

75

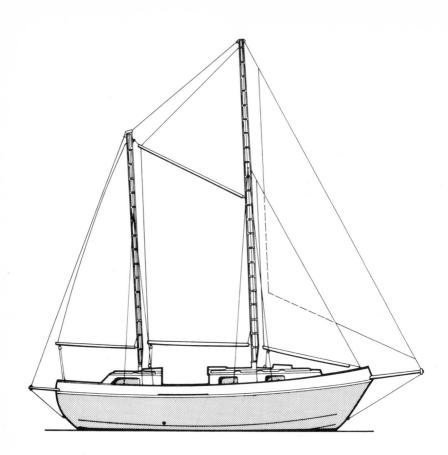

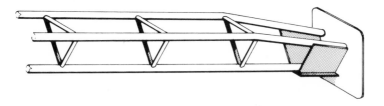

Figure 20   29-foot cruising ketch with lattice masts designed for home building by John Teal.

alongside a big ship, it is a simple matter to get a line around the truck and lower from a point above. The remainder of us, unfortunately, need some kind of derrick arrangement. There are many ways of achieving this; a ladder or a spinnaker pole could be used, but far safer to fix is this simple derrick devised by Mr Ted Broadhurst (Figure 21.)

A pair of mild steel jaws are made to fit around the outside of the mast tabernacle and drilled and bolted so that they will pivot up and down. A short section of 1 inch (25 mm) gas pipe is welded on the top of the jaws and into this conveniently slots a length of 1 inch (25 mm) electrical conduit (one is an outside

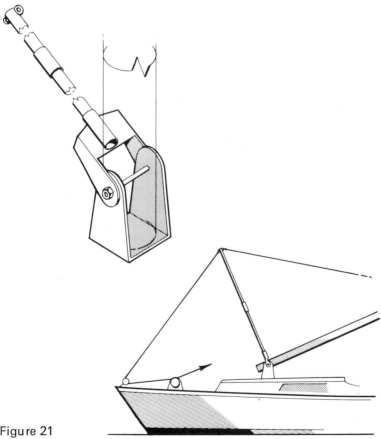

Figure 21

diameter, the other is inside – a nationalized industry oversight which works to our advantage). The derrick is made in two or more sections for convenient stowage with, once again, a short section of gas pipe welded to one to act as a joining sleeve. Two rings are welded to the upper end of the derrick pole, one to take the forestay which is shackled to it, and the other a runner which is used for heaving or lowering. The runner is taken to a winch, although a block and tackle can be used. (If you plan to do the job singlehanded then an additional safety arrangement is to extend the centre chain plates to the heights of the pivot so that the mast can be raised or lowered without letting go all the shrouds.)

Masts made from trees   The solid grown mast is the traditional mast and still is far and above the cheapest. Unpopular with modern rigs because of its weight it nevertheless remains number one with the gaff rig people. Trees suitable for masts can be obtained from the Forestry Commission for surprisingly small cost or picked up for nothing from people's gardens after a storm – they may even pay for collection! The GPO is another possible source. Almost any sound, straight tree will do.

Metal extrusions   Remember that many of the common aluminium extrusions one sees in a boat, items like toe rails, etc., can be supplied to you just the same as they are supplied to the builder. They will have to be drilled and perhaps even anodized (or painted) but need nothing too complicated to consider. See what standard aluminium sections your local stockist has to offer.

Mooring wire   The Factory Acts demand that all lift wires must be renewed every five years irrespective of their condition. The wire which is ditched, although not galvanized, is heavily impregnated with grease and makes good mooring tackle.

Motor boat under sail   The economy of fitting a displacement motor boat with a suit of sails is obvious; with these you could cross the Atlantic on a full tank of fuel. Indeed there was a time when every motor boat carried sails – they had to, the engines were so unreliable. But even today sails are a sensible precaution and would certainly reduce the demands made on the lifeboat service, the majority of whose calls come from motor boats with engine failure. But there are other sound arguments for sails too. A moderate spread of canvas in a beam or quarterly wind (the only wind directions, incidentally, in which you can ever hope to get a motor boat to sail) holds the boat steady and considerably reduces rolling, even when the engine is continuing to run. Motor-sailing means that the boat can still maintain its normal cruising speed but burn much less

Not an economy, more of a necessity. In 1942 the Royal Navy wished to send a flotilla of these boats to the West Indies. Normal fuel range would have prevented this so they were fitted with sails to carry them across the 'trade' winds. *(Photograph by kind permission of Gerald Dunkerley)*

fuel. Even a plain mizzen sail can help. It acts like a weather-cock to point the boat's head up into the wind so that she may be held comfortably while you work on an engine repair or throw a fishing line over.

Almost any motor cruiser of the displacement type can carry sail, the important thing is that the centre of effort of the sails must be kept fairly low. There was a very good article describing how to tackle the job published in *Motor Boat and Yachting*, 14 March 1975, page 56, entitled 'Switch off and sail'.

Mud berths Once you have got used to the suggestion that your new and shiny boat should be left all winter in the mud, then you will agree that it is quite a sound idea. It costs very little (in some cases nothing) and the only real objection, that the hull is being exposed to marine borers, just doesn't apply to G R P boats. Time was when almost all impoverished yachtsmen would winter their boats in this way – that was before the marinas came along and cleared away all the mud.

Some boatyards still have mud berths for rent but if you plan to pioneer and break new ground for yourself there are one or two points to ensure.

Getting permission is the first essential.The land you choose has to be owned by *someone* or come under the local authority's control. Choose a sheltered berth, one with reasonable access at most states of tide and preferably one that lies in the direction of the prevailing winds. Ensure that the bottom is soft and has no hidden obstruction.

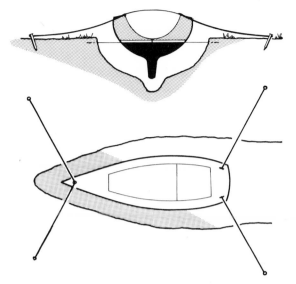

Figure 22

Once the boat is berthed you will want her to float as in-frequently as possible which means berthing at the period of equinoctial spring tides. Don't pick *the* highest tide of the year or you may never go boating again – remember that atmos-pheric pressure or long-held gale force winds make a consider-able difference to the height of the water. It is a good idea to pick the tide that you intend to berth her on and also the one you hope to float her out on before you begin; also note any intervening tides that may threaten to lift her clear of her berth so that you may be on hand.

To keep a boat in position while lying in a mud berth moor her from each quarter. The lines, which may be ropes or wires, must be sound and secured to stakes driven in the ground. It also helps to rig a length of heavy chain from the bow so that the weight will tend to pull her slightly forward if she comes afloat. The ropes should be equal to one boat's length. If your boat has a deep keel and you have the energy then it is advan-tageous to dig a trench or 'wallow' for this to sit in. Before berthing the boat, tie the four mooring lines together in the centre of the berth so that they may be picked up as one and the boat quickly secured. It is also a good idea to stake out the berth with beansticks so you will be able to recognize it as you move in.

Once in position lock the rudder so that it cannot move and become damaged. Remove all valuable items from the boat (although people who regularly winter in mud berths claim that their boats rarely attract the attention of thieves. It seems, like the owners, they show a marked reluctance to sloshing through winter-time mud.)

Navigation lamps The poorer type of navigation light can be transformed from a glimmer to a glow by the addition of kitchen foil glued to the inside. It increases reflection.

Netting One of the most seamanlike ways to stow personal gear, books and charts is to put them in netting conveniently strung beside bunks and under deckheads. The netting is soft and flexible so that the contents do not bump or slide, and what is more important, everything is so delightfully visible. Netting can be bought in several different colours and mesh sizes from gardening shops. It's much easier than fitting lockers.

Oars Practically every yacht under 22 foot could be propelled quite satisfactorily with oars and yet almost invariably we resort to engines. In France engines in small sailing boats are a rarity and most people propel their boats with oars. It's not a difference in national characteristic, simply that in France they have a tax on engines.

It is not suggested that you have to dispense with the engine altogether, just that for those odd occasions when you need to shift berths, a pair of sweeps would save the fuss and bother of rigging the outboard, not to mention the cost of the fuel.

The obvious rowing position is from the cockpit with the oarsman standing up and pushing the sweeps rather than pulling. The sweeps can fix into rowlocks on the cockpit coaming, or notches can be cut, or thole pins. Stowing the sweeps needn't present a great problem for these can lay in cradles on the cabin top and if secured in place can double as grabrails (Figure 23). *See also* YULOH.

82

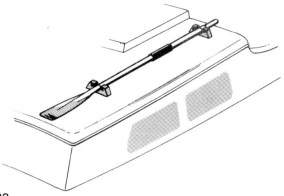

Figure 23

Oilskins The cheapest source seems to be suppliers to industry. This does not necessarily mean that your crew need have 'National Coal Board' or 'MacAlpine' stamped on their backs; there are less conspicuous kinds. If you can get an introduction then the fishermen's co-operatives are able to buy oilskins cheaply, while those supplied by Cosalts Ltd seem well recommended by everyone.

Oilskins, DIY To make your own oilskins you need a length of proofed terylene (obtainable from larger chandlery stores); some strips of Velcro; a length of wide, soft elastic; some ordinary knicker elastic; small plaited rope for draw-cords and a tin of Bostik.

Start with the trousers and use a pair of pyjama bottoms for the pattern, extended up to chest level. Leave enough for seaming top and bottom. Stitch up the legs of the trousers and put a $1\frac{1}{4}$ inch (32 mm) wide band around the waist for the draw-cord. Turn up the trouser bottoms and insert lengths of knicker elastic so that these will grip tightly on to the seaboots. The shoulder straps are made from doubled material with wide elastic inserts at the back for additional comfort. To save the trouble of sewing buttons use Velcro tabs for fastening straps at the front. The areas around the knees, seat (and elbows on the tunic) need doubling patches for additional strength and wear resistance. These are stuck on the outside with Bostik. Also

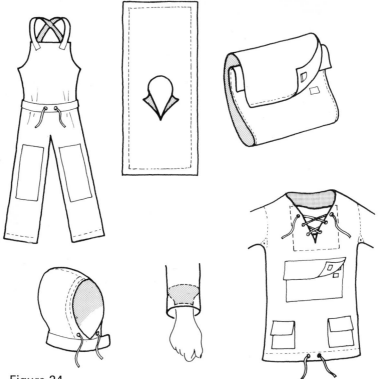

Figure 24

smear a layer of Bostik along the inside of all seams throughout the suit to make them thoroughly watertight.

The tunic is begun 'poncho' style with a large rectangular piece of material folded in half across the shoulders. Make sure that it is of generous width with an additional 1½ inches (38 mm) on either side for the seams. It should reach from shoulder to hips with sufficient for a seam at the bottom for the draw-cord. Cut a small hole in the centre of the fold for the head and then lay the material flat before deepening the neck. Next cut a slit down the neck to a depth of about 6 inches (150 mm).

The sleeves are made from parallel strips of material about 17 inches (425 mm) wide and long enough to reach from shoulder to wrist with a further 4 inches (100 mm) for a storm

84

The completed oilskins.

cuff. These are simply wide strips of soft elastic stitched to the inside of each sleeve where the top of the seam comes.

The hood is cut in profile on a double piece of material measured from the crown to the base of the neck. The two pieces are then seamed together. The face is cut away leaving enough material to turn under which will form a channel for the draw-cord. Allow $\frac{1}{2}$ inch (12 mm) for all seams on the hood. Gather in the neck and pleat into a 3 inch (75 mm) neck band which will later be double stitched on to the neck of the tunic. There is an overlap on the neck band which fastens across the chin and is held in position with Velcro.

The pockets are made separately and sewn on to the tunic. The larger one measures 14 inches (350 mm) by 9 inches (250 mm) and the smaller ones measure 10 inches (250 mm) by 8 inches (200 mm). To keep the water out effectively these are stitched on to leave a double flap. The pockets are also fastened with Velcro.

The sleeves are attached to the tunic with double seams and a gusset. The gusset is a piece of material 4 inches (100 mm) square which is first stitched to the armhole of the tunic along its two sides and then completed with the remaining two sides stitched to the sleeve opening. It has two eyelets for ventilation. Eyelets are also pressed into the neck opening for the draw-cord and there is a gusset seamed behind it.

These oilskins, from an idea by Mrs Alison Jarman, weigh just a few ounces and can easily be folded away into a small pouch.

Open boat cruising After reading the fine articles by Frank and Margaret Dye (*Yachting Monthly*, January 1968, p. 4 and January 1971, p. 102) who have sailed to all parts of the British Isles in their open boat, I am prepared to believe that this is the most exciting and perhaps the most satisfying kind of cruising. It's certainly the cheapest. The boat need never occupy a mooring, need never be craned, or stored in a boatyard; costs so little to insure, has no engine, no instruments to speak of; doesn't consume vast quantities of cordage and paint and won't take up many hours of working time – all of these things go to make it a very attractive proposition, particularly when you realize that the determined owner has a much wider choice of cruising ground – the whole of Europe and Scandinavia if he desires – since it can be trailed behind the family car. What's more he'll have the opportunity to meet so many more generous people, exposed as he is to the sleet and the rain. Not at all like the big boat cruising man who greets rain with a grimace and disappears inside his shell once again.

Of course, it's this 'shell' or rather the lack of it that does so much to keep down the costs (and is more important in this respect than the overall length of the boat). For the owner can only take items of absolute necessity: compass, bailer, primus, tent and sleeping bag, basic things like that. Just think of the redundant, luxury gear that the rest of us cart about. I'm quite convinced that the moment we put a lid on a boat our expenditure goes up by half! What I am not so sure is whether the pleasure increases by the same amount.

Outboard engines Outboard engines are considerably cheaper to buy, install and maintain than inboard units although they are usually much heavier on fuel. Still for the amount the average sailing boat uses her engine then the saving in fuel costs, when measured against capital outlay, servicing, etc., is hardly worth the effort to consider. No doubt the inboard engine makes a more efficient auxiliary but we are discussing financial merits and besides in small boats say less than 23 feet, this single benefit is submerged by a number of disadvantages. An inboard engine takes up a proportionally large space, needs the added expense and inconvenience of wiring, piping and skin fittings. It is generally inaccessible and difficult to service which means that it will probably deteriorate and depreciate far quicker than an outboard. Outboard engines unfortunately tend to get stolen so take all precautions and have them properly insured.

Paint, deck For a non-slip surface mix fine sand (or sawdust) with domestic polyurethane paint. 'Sandtex', used for painting the outside of buildings, is also suitable.

Paint, household There is absolutely no objection to using household paints both inside and outside a boat. Many people do and claim quite satisfactory results. And why not indeed when you read some of the claims of these products. Here for example is the description given on a tin of 'household' varnish: ' . . . it gives a tough, hardwearing surface which resists boiling water, hot plates, chipping and scratching, dilute household acids, alcoholic drinks, oil, etc. . . . it is flexible and does not crack or flake under pressure'.

But not only can 'household' paints be used; some of the paints developed for the building industry are highly suitable. Take 'Structoplast' for example. This is an epoxy-rich formula which requires no catalyst and is used in the building trade principally as a damp-proof membrane. However, it has also been used in harbour installations as protection against damp and corrosion and is said to be resistant to sea water and alkalis. 'Structoplast' is applied with a brush and gives a black, glossy finish, which remains flexible enough to counter hair cracks and may be overpainted with any colour. It doesn't melt in high temperatures so it cannot get sticky on the hands and feet, and is used for protection of wood, metal and concrete!

Another industrial paint is 'Synthaprufe', sold as a domestic anti-damp remedy. One man used it to paint the bottom of his boat and discovered it had remarkable anti-fouling properties. (*See also* ANTI-FOULING.)

Don't go to the expense of painting the interior surface of a GRP hull with anything other than ordinary emulsion paint; it's what most of the builders use.

Paint removers   Proprietary paint strippers contain very strong solvents which are also highly volatile, so they boil off quickly. The evaporation however can be slowed down – and the paint stripper made to go further – if the area is covered with kitchen foil made up into foot squares. Apply the stripper, cover with foil, leave for ten minutes then peel off and scrape away. Paint removers can also be used to rejuvenate old brushes which have solidified. Soak them for a couple of days, working the bristles occasionally, and then give a final clean-up with a wire brush.

Paint remover substitute   If you can get hold of any sugar soap then this is one of the best and cheapest paint removers. Something which is commonly available from hardware shops is caustic soda; mixed with water this makes a good paint remover and is used in the antique trade for stripping pinewood furniture. It works out about 10p per gallon. I use it exclusively – although with considerable caution; caustic soda is a hazardous preparation. If you are using it then always have a bucket of water handy to neutralize splashes etc. Apply with a sponge tied to a stick or rope yarn brush (*opposite*). Rubber gloves are also advisable. A handful of caustic in a gallon of water is the approximate measure (always add caustic to water, not water to caustic). Brush over an area of several square feet and allow to soak for a little while. This should be sufficient to remove the top layer of paint. Scrape away and repeat the operation successively until you arrive at the bare wood. Rinse well in fresh water to neutralize caustic before re-painting.

88

Paint (rust prevention)   The quality of paint has improved immeasurably over the years as the return of an immaculate *British Steel* from her circumnavigation testified. Twenty years ago nobody connected with ships and boats would ever have thought it possible that a steel-hulled vessel could ever have sailed so many miles without even a smudge of rust on her sides. Indeed the quality of these paints brings into question the traditional idea that all fittings and deck gear must be made from non-corrosive materials, or galvanized. It has been found that if mild steel is cleaned well, treated with 'Kurust', 'Metalife' or one of the other phosphoric paints and then given two coats of 'Galvafroid', it stands up well to sea conditions.

Paint scraper   A small piece of glass makes a most efficient scraper and is particularly good for cleaning up wood prior to sandpapering. One square of glass gives eight razor-sharp

Two home-made brushes. The one on the left with copper pipe handle is suitable for gluing and resin jobs. Instead of cleaning you simply cut off the end and slide more rope through. The rope yarn brush on the right is handy for sweeping up or washing the dishes.

edges which, as soon as they become blunt, are simply discarded. It sounds far more dangerous to use than it in fact is; I have never yet cut myself.

Paint skins   The skin that forms on paint that has been stored is wasteful. It is also very difficult to remove without breaking it into miniscule pieces which submerge only to reappear on your paintwork. To prevent this it is advisable to clean the edges of the lid and tin after use and store upside down. However, if this means you have to hang like a hibernating bat just to read the contents then a better suggestion is to cut a disc of waxed paper (use the tin lid as a template) and drop this on the

top of the paint before storing. The paper denies the air contact with the paint which causes the skin to form.

Paraffin Paraffin is the pensioner's fuel. Every winter a million old souls in knitted shawls and tartan slippers snuggle up to their oil stoves and warm their bowls of porridge. A heavy tax or increase in the price of paraffin would be tantamount to genocide; no government would ever dare to do it.

So, as long as you don't feel bad about running your boat on the old folks' subsidized fuel you can confidently expect that paraffin will always be far and above the cheapest fuel.

Paraffin engines At present prices – and the differential grows wider – a paraffin engine costs less than half as much to run as a petrol engine, although the unit itself is slightly more expensive. It is not so economical as a diesel engine but then the paraffin engine is much cheaper to buy initially. Other advantages which the paraffin engine has over diesel is that it is much less noisy, not so heavy and available in smaller sizes. Its distinct advantage over petrol, apart from price, is that it is much less of a fire risk.

The disadvantages of the paraffin engine are that the fuel is not so readily available and that the engine itself demands more attention if it is to run satisfactorily. The sump oil needs changing and the spark plugs need cleaning more frequently, that sort of thing. It used to be grumbled that the fuel had an unpleasant smell, but compared with diesel that can hardly be so.

Most paraffin engines start (and stop) on petrol and some engines are equipped with a dual carburettor for the purpose. Paraffin is a less volatile fuel and requires to be kept properly vaporized from leaving the carburettor until it arrives at the spark plug. If this is not achieved then the engine may fail to start or run unevenly, causing droplets of unburnt fuel to find their way down into the cylinder bores and into the lubricating oil (which is why this needs to be changed more often). However, by warming the engine initially by starting and running on petrol these troubles are prevented. So long as this is done properly and a good working temperature maintained, most of the paraffin engine's traditional troubles are eliminated. Certainly modern ones are much better than old models.

There are several paraffin engines currently available. There is the small Watermota Shrimp, a single cylinder four-stroke power unit of 147 c.c. This is fitted with a 4:1 reduction gear and a variable pitch reversing propeller. It it particularly suitable as a yacht auxiliary as it is air cooled which eliminates water pump, skin fittings and water circulation system. Although this unit has a petrol version the paraffin engine accounts for 95 per cent of home sales. A larger engine is the Brit 10 h.p. two-cylinder unit and an even larger engine is the four-cylinder MB20B from Volvo Penta. This engine has a rating of 42 h.p. at 3000 r.p.m. Another paraffin engine is the Wickstrom two-cylinder W-2 manufactured by the Vasa Motor AB of Finland and marketed here by Wickstrom Marine Limited.

Yamaha make a paraffin outboard motor marketed by E. P. Barrus Ltd, who also sell a paraffin conversion kit for each of the Johnson range. It is claimed that the cost of the kit for the larger 40 h.p. engine is completely paid for by reduced fuel costs by the time 100 hours have been run. On a 20 h.p. outboard the pay-off comes around 150 hours. The kit includes a special carburettor which automatically mixes the petrol and paraffin, a separate paraffin tank and a thicker cylinder head gasket to lower the compression ratio of the engine. It is said that the engine runs perfectly on any commercial grade of paraffin and the kit, which has been perfected and built by the Army, takes about an hour to fit. (The marketing company, unfortunately, are very slack in answering letters.)

So far as I can determine there is only one company which offers vaporizing equipment for the conversion of inboard petrol engines; they are Leigh Marine, 14 Queen's Avenue, Leigh-on-Sea, Essex. They produce the GMS vaporizer which fits the Ford 100E engine. This unit is perhaps the cheapest 'ready to fit' car engine available and has been widely adopted for marine conversion. Currently the vaporizer and gaskets cost £20·00; a modified carburettor jet plug with drain tap costs £2·50; a two-way fuel assembly costs £3·00, and a sump pump kit costs £6·00. The company also supply the basic engine and all marinizing components.

In his book *Marine Conversions* (Adlard Coles), Nigel Warren shows how other petrol engines can be converted to paraffin and claims that with the bigger units the fuel bill can be cut by two-thirds!

Paraffin lighting   I could suggest that an oil lamp in a boat gives atmosphere, the very kind of atmosphere that some of these ornate electric lamps try to create. However let's stick to the practicalities. If you want to save the worry and expense of wiring, fittings, bulbs, switches, batteries (and charging circuits in most cases) then paraffin lamps are something to consider. A few of the bulkhead fitting type give a good background light although a Tilley lamp is necessary for reading (I reckon it's as bright as a forty watt bulb.) Navigation side lights also have to be paraffin but it is recommended that you have the Tilley lamp handy in the cabin, lit but dimmed, ready to exhibit as a stern light in accordance with the Collision Regulations. Soaking paraffin wicks in strong vinegar gives a brighter light; it also prevents smoking.

Paraffin stoves   There is little argument that paraffin is the cheapest fuel for cooking and certainly one of the safest. The only drawback is the business of pre-heating which although not dangerous (the secret of success is to pre-heat thoroughly) can be a nuisance. Use the spring-clip and wick pre-heaters as sold with Tilley lamps; it's much easier than trying to decant methylated spirits into the reservoir.

A good collection of oven, cookers and cabin heaters, including the Taylor Para-Fin range is stocked by MacAlister Carvall Ltd, Stem Lane, New Milton, Hants.

Parallel rules   A suitable pair of parallel rules can be made from two tufnol sail battens joined, as shown in Figure 25, by two lengths of braided line. A deluxe version employs Perspex which has the benefit of being transparent and upon which the bearing lines can be scribed.

Another idea is a simplification of the roller type of parallel rules which is simply to use a short length of dowel or broom-

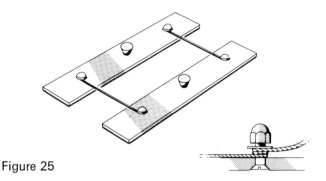

Figure 25

stick. It's a sound arrangement for a boat where the conventional rules can be difficult to use. To prevent it from skidding put tubular steel chair rubbers (obtainable from ironmongers) on the ends or alternatively walking stick rubbers. In all events make sure you have a matching pair otherwise your ruler will describe large circles.

Penetrating oil A good substitute is diesel oil; some people claim it is better than the real thing. Diesel is also good for shifting rust, so if you have a fitting which is gummed up soak it in a bowl of diesel.

Preservatives One of the best-known boats on the east coast is *Fanny of Cowes*. She was built before the turn of the century and still regularly competes in the Old Gaffers' Association Races. Not infrequently she wins them. The secret of her everlasting youth is claimed to be that before she was built her owner instructed that every item of timber be soaked in linseed oil to preserve it.

Nowadays such a thing would be prohibitively expensive (and you have to live about eighty years to enjoy the benefit) but John Leather, who apart from being a Lloyd's surveyor also builds the odd wooden boat, suggests that a mixture of one part linseed oil to two parts paraffin applied liberally reduces the expense but still makes an extremely good preservative. I've tried it and found it to be excellent; it costs just a little more than

94

a third of the price of proprietary brand preservatives. Take your own tin and buy your linseed oil from a builder's merchant.

Propeller A propeller with bent or damaged blades results in increased fuel consumption. There are firms which advertise in yachting magazines who fair up propellers at a fraction of the cost of a new one. A correctly matched propeller and engine is also important if fuel savings are to be made.

Protection against wear It was said the biggest single expenditure in a sailing ship was the replacement of gear weakened or destroyed by chafe. It was reckoned to work out more than the crew's food and wages! Of course there is no comparison between those old hay waggons and the modern sailing boat, but nonetheless just how much of our gear meets a premature end due to undetected wear? Sheets, for example, are particularly vulnerable, especially where they pass through a lead block. To reduce this localized wear it is a good idea to cut them longer than required and splice the sail fastening off centre. Then before the first signs of wear at the blocks become too marked it is expedient to cut a foot off the shorter end of the sheet and shift the fastening so that the wear is moved progressively.

Figure 26

The lower part and bottom splice in a shroud or stay is subject to more weathering than the top part (particularly prone is galvanized rigging). Turn all rigging end for end each season, the same with halyards where possible and especially anchor cable. Warps that may be subject to 'sawing' with the movement of the boat can be protected by passing them through a short length of plastic tube and securing this at the fairlead. Tennis balls, split then sewn at the extremity of the mast spreaders, cut down the wear in the bigger headsails. Look for signs of chafe wherever it is suspected, it could be adding dramatically to your boating costs (Figure 26).

Quick release fitting This can be made simply by sawing across two links of chain and filing both cuts into V-shapes (Figure 27.)

Figure 27

Radar reflector The model shown can be made in a variety of practical sizes from 8 inches (200 mm) up to 18 inches (450 mm). Its American inventor, Robert Wendt, says that although the smaller one is quite adequate, the size of the echo increases dramatically with the size of the reflector. In tests he found that the 8 inch (200 mm) model gave an echo equivalent to a navigation buoy while the larger 12 inch (300 mm) model was found equal to that of a 75 foot (23 m) fishing boat! It is made from 1·5 or 2 mm aluminium sheet. The construction is much easier to understand if you first make a small-sized paper model. Cut the parts shown in Figure 28 and assemble them in this order: Part 1 goes into Part 2; Part 3 slides in next and Part 4, the locking piece, through the slot marked E which is then bolted at C.Ci and D.Di to hold the whole thing together.

96

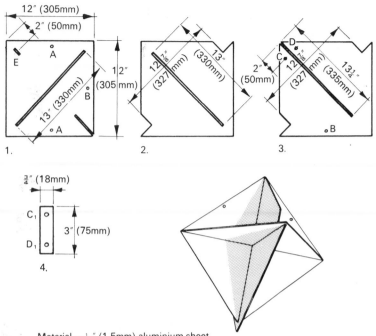

Material – $\frac{1}{16}$" (1.5mm) aluminium sheet

Figure 28

When the reflector is properly assembled, the suspension holes marked B are on adjacent faces of one corner. If a line is rove through each of these and tied to a ring to form a bridle the reflector can be hoisted at the proper tilt so that radar beams strike squarely into the corners. The holes marked A are for guy lines so that it doesn't swing or spin wildly when hoisted aloft on a flag halyard or whatever.

Radio direction finder It is possible to make cheap and effective radio direction finder from a transistor radio, a handbearing compass and a few bits and pieces. The method was described by Mr A. Fox-Green (who is a wizard at making cheap marine instruments and ought to write a book on the subject) and published in *Practical Boatowner,* July 1970, page 67.

Experienced people maintain that if the sail is to retain the correct shape reef points are essential. For it's the knowledge of where and how tight to tie them that eliminates the wrinkles and hard spots. This too is why the lead of the leach pendant is so important. It has to be very slightly astern of the place where the leach cringle would fall naturally. In other words the aim is to stretch the sail aft. There are special snap fittings sold to secure the reef cringles on to the boom but it is cheaper to use the traditional rope lashing.

Reefing headsails   At first aquaintance this may not sound very practical but it's a traditional idea; working craft often had reefed headsails and would sometimes tie up a few reef points along the foot for better visibility (those with deck-scraping genoas might copy this idea). Indeed the principle of reefed headsails has been adopted recently in racing boats with the 'blast reacher' which becomes both the number two and the number three genoas! The surplus sail seems to cause no embarrassment when reefed and simply lies on the deck, although some owners like it secured with lacing lines or reef points. So, if you haven't yet completed your sail wardrobe then think about a 'blast reacher'; it could save you buying an extra sail.

Figure 31

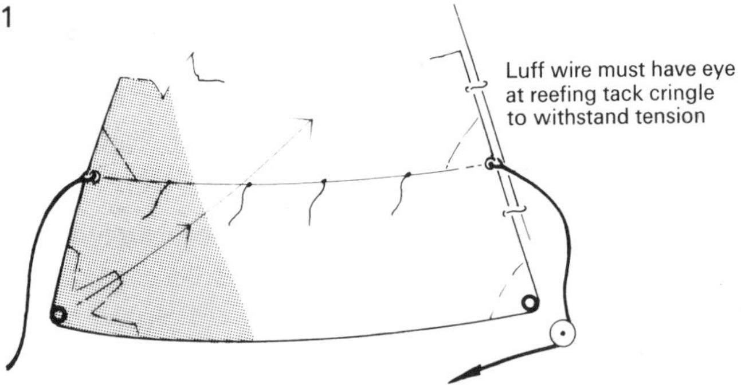

Luff wire must have eye at reefing tack cringle to withstand tension

Reefing arrangement for genoa

Alternatively, a medium heavy weight genoa can be made into a reefing sail with the provision of additional cringles, reinforcing, reefing points.

Resale value This is a long-term economy. The man who is building or buying a boat today should always have an eye to the future . . . to the day when he has to sell the thing, buy another boat or augment his old-age pension. The sage advice is the same now as it always was; buy a boat from a good yard and the pen of a good designer. As an adjunct to this choose a middle-of-the-road design rather than something fashionable or outlandish. There will always be eager buyers for Folkboats, Vertues, Dragons and the well-established GRP designs; yachtsmen are very conservative.

For the man who is building his own boat the advice about a good design still applies. But whatever design you build and in whatever material it is important to concentrate on the style and quality of the finish. So long as the boat has a good finish and looks pretty she will sell; when the yachtsman isn't being conservative he's a sucker for appearance.

Rigging screws, DIY A superior, though less attractive, rigging screw can be made from a section of steel rod, bent into

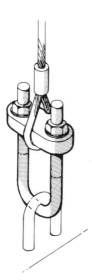

Figure 32

Rigging screws

Types of rigging screws used by the Post Office. The bottom thread needs to be sawn short and re-fashioned. (Notice the type of splice in right-hand photograph.)

a U-shape, threaded and galvanized. A piece of steel plate, notched in the middle to locate the shroud eye, is drilled and dropped over the threads to be held down by a couple of nuts (Figure 32). It's a better arrangement than the 'bottle' type which is prone to hidden rust, needs a locking device to prevent it walking back and is inherently weaker. It is weaker because the weight is taken only on one thread, the one at the top and the one at the bottom, and if either of these strip you've had it!

Rigging screws, factory-built The cheapest bought-in rigging screw is the galvanized one from the agricultural supplier (*see* CHANDLERY). An even cheaper but less immediate source is the Post Office. They use rigging screws to stay telegraph poles and since overhead lines are being phased out there should be quite a few coming up on the second-hand market! (*See also* FENCE-STRAINERS *and* DEADEYES.)

Rope Don't be seduced by the sunny charm of synthetic rope; natural fibre ropes have been doing the job perfectly well for

102

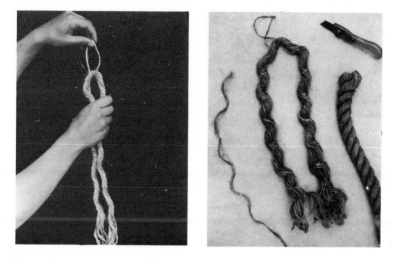

Yarns from old rope make cheap and expendable lashings.
Make into bights and pull out from centre.

centuries and nothing has come along to change that. You
probably won't buy *new* natural fibre rope because it's
expensive but lengths of ex-Government manila are frequently
advertised in magazines and make adequate mooring warps.

Rope deteriorates through the wear and abrasion on its
outside surface. So if you have two ropes to do the same job
and one is bigger then this one should last longer because surface
area is greater and the wear therefore more diffused. What it
means is that there is disproportionately less wear in a larger
rope employed for the same job. For this reason it becomes a
sound economy to buy a larger but cheaper quality of rope
than, say, a superior but thinner one. And furthermore a large
rope is much easier to handle than a thin one.

But the advantage goes still further if you are prepared to use
bigger-sized ropes for such things as halyards, topping lifts, etc.,
because you can achieve a certain standardization. And if you
can do this then you save money by buying rope in long single
lengths, rather than little bits of varying thicknesses. A 600 foot
coil of rope can be as much as 30 per cent cheaper than
equivalent ropes purchased in short lengths of different sizes.

103

Where possible buy ropes supplied to the road haulage industry and people like that.

Rope boarding ladder   These really are so very simple to make (Figure 33) that it is a mere extravagance to buy the ready-made item. Place a length of lead piping at the bottom to ensure the rungs hang vertically into the water.

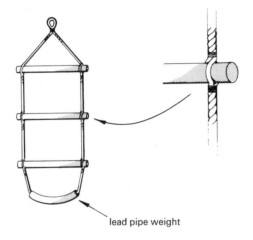

lead pipe weight

Figure 33

Safety harness   Safety equipment is such a sensitive subject one hesitates to recommend anything but the most expensive. Still come the day we can look upon life and death in a more philosophical way, perhaps I'll be able to say buy webbing and hooks from the army and navy shop and make your own safety harness. They won't carry the 'kite mark' but at least they are better than nothing.

Sails, DIY   There can't be any better advice on this subject than to recommend you to read *Make Your Own Sails* by Bowker and Budd. It's a modest-priced publication now in its eighth edition. The recognized work, it has helped thousands of people to make their own sails including some well known ocean-going yachtsmen. The book can be bought direct from Bowker and Budd Ltd, Bosham, Sussex.

Materials for home-made sails vary according to taste and size. In small boats, dinghies, etc., good quality bedsheets have been used while unbleached cotton from a draper's shop is also considered to be suitable. Certainly cotton is easier to work, cheaper to buy and, because the threads bed neatly into the material, much less prone to chafe. Terylene can be bought from large chandleries and some sailmakers also sell it. At least one man has used flat-fibre polypropylene cloth which is cheaper and much stronger than terylene. Unfortunately it is not ultra-violet proof and needs protecting from sunlight when not in use.

Sails, dressing   The traditional sail dressing which is a mixture of red ochre and fish oil is now both expensive and virtually unobtainable. So instead, why not use Rentokil's 'Cedarwood', which is sold as a timber preservative? The skipper of the seventy-seven-year-old barge *Lord Roberts* claims that this lasts longer, gives a better colour, leaves the material more supple and is easier to apply. Those who make their own sails from un-bleached cotton or calico may find this an altogether more attractive and colourful proposition than some of the usual waterproofing agents.

Sails, second-hand   While second-hand sails can be bought direct, most lofts prefer to dispose of old stock through an agency. This can be understood when, having dragged a bundle from the back of the shelf, spread it out on the floor and swept away the mould and the mice droppings, the customer – who will never spend more than a couple of quid – decides that he doesn't want it! After one or two experiences like that the sail-maker and the private vendor happily pay the agency's small commission.

Therefore if you wish to get hold of a wardrobe of second-hand sails which require the minimum of recutting send the exact details to an agency such as Resails Ltd, 6 Old Coastguards Road, Felpham, Bognor Regis (the names and addresses of other agencies can be found in the yachting magazines). As a price guide this agency says that a second-hand sail in first class condition will sell for about half the price of a new one. No commission is charged to the buyer and collection in most cases is arranged between seller and buyer.

Damaged sails can often be snapped up on the first gusty day of Cowes Week!

Sailing tender You have no need to buy a specially designed sailing dinghy for those odd afternoon sails from the moorings. The average yacht's tender can be converted to sail quite easily and most importantly the gear can be stowed inside the boat and set up in a jiffy.

The most popular conversion is the standing lug (although a sprit rig is good and carries more sail). For this the mast does not have to be stayed and both it and the sail can be handed and set in the same operation. The conversion shown in Figure 35 was contrived by Des Sleightholme, editor of *Yachting Monthly*. It was specifically made for an 8-foot tender but boats up to 15 foot have been successfully converted.

The gear required is as follows. The pine mast and bamboo yard should each be about 8 feet long and just short enough to stow inside the dinghy. The mast should be roughly 2 inches in diameter and have a brass bolt drilled down inside the truck and protruding slightly; this is to hold the yard becket. The bamboo pole may be obtained from a carpet warehouse. It should have two rope beckets, the second for use when reefed should be one-third down from the peak. The sail is made from unbleached calico bought from a draper's, although a good-quality bedsheet could be used, suitably waterproofed with a substance such as Nev. The sail measurements are roughly: head = 7 ft 6 in. (2·3 m), leach = 8 ft 6 in. (2·6 m), foot = 6 ft (1·8 m), luff = 4 ft (1·2 m). Foot and leach should be taped for strength but head and luff must have a boltrope sewn in. Cringles can either be sewn in or brass eyelets used. There should be one at the tack, one at the claw and two reef cringles also. Smaller cringles along the head enable it to be laced to the yard.

A leeboard is made from a $\frac{5}{16}$ inch (8 mm) marine ply and should measure 3 ft (1·0 m) by 18 in. (450 mm). A small block of wood fixed to the inboard side will allow it to rest on the gun-

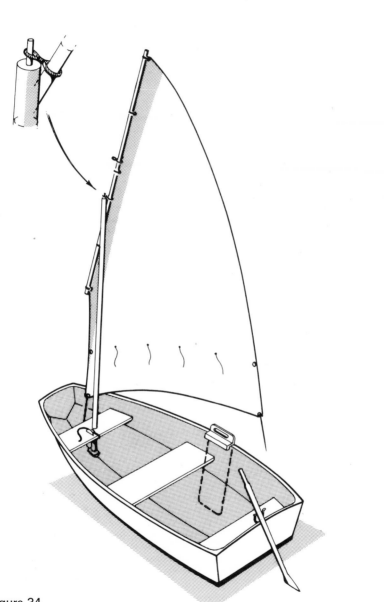

Figure 34

wale while a lanyard fixed around the thwart will keep it in position. The leeboard is always rigged on the leeward side where the pressure of water holds it rock solid against the boat's side.

The mast is stepped through a hole in the foward thwart and into a step bonded or screwed on top of the keelson. Steering is by means of an oar and for this a sculling notch or rowlock must be fitted in the transom. The tack line is secured by passing it under the thwart and on to a clam cleat.

Mr Sleightholme remarks, 'The magical thing about this rig is that if you let fly the tack line the whole contrivance up-ends and dissolves into a mass of floppy folds so that if a hard squall descends one can just jerk the line and duck.'

Thomas Foulkes Ltd sell sailing conversion kits.

Sailor's clothes peg   Made from sail twine and cowhitched to the garment . . . the harder it blows the tighter it grips!

Figure 35

Cheap fishing dinghy built by Mr Gerald Hammond. It was built with exterior plywood on frames which were second-hand floorboards. The spars and oars came from old white pine floorboards and the shrouds are made from fencing wire. The mainsail is a recut headsail from a larger boat and the nails are galvanized roofing nails. The entire boat cost less than £40 when built and has been in use for the past three seasons.
(Photograph: Steven Hammond)

Sandpaper Buy it by the sleeve. This can save up to as much as a third of the price as buying sheets separately.

Sea water Away from harbour the fresh water supply can be saved by washing dishes in sea water. Don't wash clothes because this can give you dhobi's itch. You can wash yourself of course, using sea-water soap.

Self-steering gear Quantock Marine Enterprises of Bridgwater, Somerset supply a kit wind vane system which is currently priced at £52. An independent test carried out by *Yachting Monthly* showed that it gives quite satisfactory results in winds force 3 and above, although some tuning is necessary. It takes about two hours to put together.

There are several other designs for complete home construction. Colin Mudie has a very simple one, and from time to time some inspired DIY man publishes his experiments in a yachting magazine. One such was published in *Yachting Monthly*, May 1974, page 627. Another design, this time for a motor boat, appeared in *Practical Boatowner*, March 1970, page 49.

Sextants, bubble These surprisingly cheap sextants were designed for use aboard aircraft. They have an artificial horizon which permits sights to be taken at night or when the sea horizon is not visible. In the original state as sold they are of very little use aboard a small boat because of the difficulty of keeping the bubble steady with the boat's motion; they are reasonably accurate in slight sea conditions but quite hopeless when the sea becomes lively. It is possible, however, to buy these sextants converted to marine use or you can do it yourself (see the article published by Mr Fox-Green in *Practical Boatowner*, November 1970, page 38).

Sextants, plastic These are ideally suitable for use aboard a boat; they are robust and about one-tenth the price of the proper job. Two important points to remember about their use, however, is that the mirrors may not be sealed, so they need to be washed in fresh water each time after use. The other point is that the material is not as resistant to the effect of temperature as brass and therefore it is necessary to keep it out of the sun as much as possible and check for index and side error each time it is used. These small considerations apart there are plenty of experienced navigators to vouch for the dependency of the plastic sextant which on ocean voyages has been found to give an accuracy to within two or three miles.

Shackle pin lanyard A small lanyard secured to the eye of the pin may not be the most novel idea but it does save buying shackles with retaining pins which are infinitely more expensive (Figure 36).

Figure 36

Sharing Undoubtedly the best way to cut costs is to share a boat and its expenses. Some partnerships have endured for years, others founder at the first sign of damage; as an arrangement it is not without its hazards. Choose a partner wisely, more for his aptitude for hard work and fairmindedness than his boating abilities. It isn't necessary to sail together; indeed some of the best partnerships work on a time-share basis. Get an agreement drawn up legally and decide how long it will run (best to do it on a year-to-year basis). Then, to save solicitor's time and your money, agree first between yourselves the many points you wish this to cover, which should include such forgotten items as how the sixty-four shares which every vessel comprises might be disposed of in the event of one partner's abdication – or death; and whether these should be sold at original cost or current value. See that a proper inventory is included so there is no later argument as to who bought what and who it belongs to. Take out a large third party insurance and decide how damage or loss not covered by insurance will be paid for – is the man who occasioned it to pay or will it be a joint responsibility? Consider at the outset how the mooring fees and maintenance costs will be appropriated. Have it understood that whoever uses the boat will have it fuelled and watered afterwards; there is no quicker way to end a partnership than for the next person to arrive and find an empty fuel tank on a Friday night. Try to work out some sort of work appropriation.

If you are to sail the boat separately, draw up a calendar as to who has the boat each weekend with arrangements for annual holidays. Come to an agreement too about the friends you may invite and whether one or other partner may lend the boat to any of them.

This may sound dreadfully pedestrian when there is the exciting prospect of two life-long friends pooling their savings to buy a boat but do get these things legally ironed out; it saves argument and it's too late for misunderstandings and ambiguities afterwards.

Personalities are the great problem and it's a hard fact of life that while two men can get along admirably the same can rarely be said of their wives. Low maintenance boats are a safer bet for shared ownership because it's work-sharing that can cause the most friction. One partner may have more time to devote than another, or he might live closer, or be more skilled. There is nothing like thinking that you are working harder on the boat than your partner to create bad feeling. The alternative of putting the work in the hands of the yard may be more expensive but at least there can be no argument about paying their bills.

Racing men and cruising men do not make the best partners; arguments as to what is *essential* gear will be interminable, while a racing fixture will almost certainly clash with the other's annual cruise. Then again racing invariably means strained or broken gear which is another bone of contention. Other partner-

112

ships unlikely to endure are those where there is a wide disparity of income or age, bachelors with men with large families, and the happy-go-lucky type with the meticulous and pedantic. The best chances are between two racing enthusiasts or a novice and master relationship – until the novice becomes too knowing, that is. But said to be the very best arrangement of all is to share a boat with a vicar. Not only is he likely to be an honest and fair-minded sort of individual but he would leave the boat free on Sunday.

You can always advertise for a vicar, or anybody else come to that, in the classified section of the yachting magazines.

Ship's name The professional way to signwrite today seems to be one of the dry-transfer products such as Letrasign. These are self-adhesive vinyl letters which you see everywhere from railway stations to aircraft fuselages. Alternatively you can buy Letraset and varnish over the top of it. There is a great versatility in Letraset with styles ranging from Times Roman to Gothic and Old English. You can even buy the decorative scrollwork to go with it. Letraset is obtainable from large stationers or art-suppliers.

Shower A cheap shower, and one that uses the minimum amount of water, can be got by using an old portable garden weed sprayer. Simply fill up the canister with a gallon or so of hot water, pump up the pressure with the handle and then slip away to some undisturbed place for your shower.

Sink Not only does the ordinary washing up bowl (deep square pattern) make a perfectly good sink and save you the cost of plumbing and skin fittings, but it can easily be lifted from its place in the galley (a recess cut into the working top) and taken outside for someone else to wash up. Or do it yourself in the sunset.

Skin fittings There is an old maxim which says the less holes in the hull the better. If at the design stage you consider such things as air-cooled or outboard engines, chemical toilets and

113

utilizing openings already there, like the rudder trunk or the centreboard case for cockpit drains and galley waste, then not only do you reduce the number of holes but you save on plumbing costs and skin fittings also. Transom pipes for cockpit drains are another consideration.

In the last few years nylon skin fittings have come on to the market. They are cheaper than those of brass or phosphor bronze; reports suggest they are quite satisfactory.

Sounding pole A bamboo pole, painted to keep out the wet and the weather and ringed with red paint at the boat's draught, is very much quicker than the leadline for ascertaining the depth in shallow water and, if a lot of sounding has to be done, very much kinder on the hands. (Its superiority over the echosounder doesn't even merit discussion!) A sounding pole when not in use can, like a boathook and oars, be secured in cradles on the cabin top and take on the job of a handrail.

Stanchions These can be made up from 1 inch (25 mm) water pipe with a steel plate welded on the bottom. Use wedge-shaped pads of wood to ensure the correct angle and walking stick ferrules as capping.

Hilyard yachts always have galvanized water pipe for their guardrails and stanchions.

Station pointer Horizontal angles obtained with a (plastic) sextant are not the most popular way to fix a small boat's position but they are easily the most accurate. They eliminate compass error and the handling errors which can so often result from the use of a small bearing compass in a boat. Simply all that is required are three clear objects on the shore and a station pointer with which to transfer the angles so measured between the objects on to the chart. The economy here is to do away with the station pointer and draw the angles on tracing paper. Tracing paper is cheap to make; just soak ordinary paper in linseed oil and hang it somewhere to dry.

Storm jib This is one of those items that a sailing man has to buy although he'll rarely, if ever, use it. There is no possibility of saving here but you get a better return on your money if you follow Hoods the sailmaker's suggestion and use it as a staysail. They recommend that in breezy conditions a good storm jib with a wire luff can be rigged as a staysail on the mast with a spare halyard, such as the spinnaker's for example. The sail is tacked down hard at about mid-point on the foredeck and adjusted so that it can be sheeted inside the rigging for close-windward work.

Stove The old solid fuel stove from a caravan is one of the cheapest boat heaters available. It's also one of the cheeriest. Furthermore it circulates the air more efficiently than most and is the only one that makes toast and burns driftwood.

For those who sail in a smokeless zone then an inverted clay flower pot on the galley cooker makes a reasonable cabin heater. Mind how you lift it off.

Surplus weight For better fuel economy in a motor boat don't carry surplus weight. Unnecessary amounts of fuel and water, old gear, etc., cost money to move about.

Survey This may not sound much of an economy but with all these dreadful people building boats in exterior plywood and making sails with bedsheets, the rest of us can't be too careful.

115

Wooden boats especially should be surveyed. Most of them are now upwards of fifteen years old and that is a critical period in their lifetime. The increase in the numbers of mysterious founderings of wooden boats is believed by many to be due to undetected faults and weaknesses.

In almost every case the money spent on the survey fee is recouped when the inevitable defects have to be put right by the owner (or he has to drop his asking price). Then again a survey may condemn a boat outright, and just think of the money that saves.

A good tip when buying a boat is to pick out three examples of a type you like, and about the same price, and limit them all to the same area. Then ask a local surveyor to make an *inspection*, of all three, and to tell you which he considers the best. The arrangement is cheap, gives a wide cover and although no substitute for a proper survey it may just be that the surveyor is so impressed by his choice that he considers a survey unnecessary....

Tack downhaul This can be dispensed with on smaller craft with the provision of a tack line and toggles (Figure 37). This makes use of a length of pre-stretched terylene and a thimble eye shackled to the stemhead fitting. Using it the foresails can be set by swigging on the halyard and if coloured whippings on the halyard are used to correspond with each sail then the correct tensioning is established.

The choice of set tack lengths which the arrangement provides means also that the sheet lead block does not have to be repositioned for each sail. Thus it does away with the genoa track and slide (*see* GENOA TRACK AND SLIDE).

Tax concession If you can prove that your boat is in some way essential to your earnings then expenses can be claimed against income tax.

Thimbles can be made up from old handles of galvanized buckets.

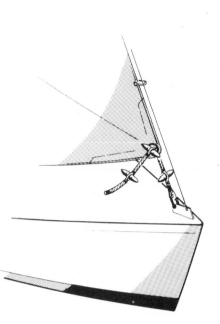

Figure 37

Tides Motor-boat men who use the tides as friends save themselves a quantitative amount in fuel. Think of it; a moderate three-knot tide can, over a period of three hours, mean a difference of eighteen miles – depending on whether you go with it or go against it.

Timber Furniture auctions produce some excellent timber for boatbuilding, and of a like you may not be able to purchase elsewhere. Make sure before bidding that it's solid stuff and not simply veneered.

Demolition contractors may be another good source especially when they are pulling down a house of quality or a church with pitchpine beams and pews. Ship breakers are certainly worth a visit.

Heavy machinery parts often come in large wooden packing cases which may later become an embarrassment outside the factory door. A man with a sledge hammer and pick-up truck might just be an answer to a prayer. The wood is good at least for a building shed and perhaps some temporary framing.

Timber house builders, cabinet makers and joinery factories sometimes have generous-sized offcuts, which could be made up into laminates. Look out for timber used in beach defence work, piers and wharves; some of it is very good hardwood.

Finally, if you do have to buy your timber, especially hardwood, go to a country sawmill rather than a timber importer. English elm is cheaper than imported softwood.

Towing a dinghy   is an extravagant way of burning fuel – stow it, don't tow it.

Trade prices   If you propose to build a boat, which is a protracted and expensive project, then right at the start go to your local timber supplier and ask to open a trade account. Point out to them that you propose to spend perhaps many hundreds of pounds which must equal, if not exceed, the business placed by many of his smaller trade customers. Some timber suppliers also sell hardware so that glues, fastenings and paints can also be bought at a discount.

Trailers   Rather than buy a trailer that you may only use twice a year and which for the rest of the time lies deteriorating and blocking up your driveway, it might be cheaper to hire one. (See *Boat World* for hirers.)

Trailers can also be made from kits (see *Boat World* again) or you can build one suitable for a load of four tons from a pair of Mini sub frames. An article published in *Practical Boatowner*, January 1971, page 57, shows how to do it.

Trenails   or trun'ls they used to be called – simply hardwood wedges or dowels used in wooden boat construction. As fastenings for the hog and keel they were ideal, inexpensive and not prone to corrosion; it was said that trenails made of oak lasted longer than iron.

You can buy the modern equivalent – dowels – in packets already splined with glue channels from the DIY shop, or you can make up yourself; either way don't ignore them.

Usage Paradoxically the more use you make of your boat the cheaper your boating becomes. Being aboard more often and for longer periods you can keep her better maintained and thus save on expensive repair jobs. You are safe from the temptations of shore life, the fleshpots, the restaurants and racetracks, the shops and the never-ending round of car journeys. You can still entertain on board but in a less lavish style, and then again it's quite reasonable to expect friends to bring their own food aboard. The boat should take the place of expensive overseas holidays or 'Winterbreak Weekends' and 'Away-Days'. In fact some lucky people might be able to move aboard permanently for periods and put their house up for summer rent.

Wander lead This is a very adaptable piece of equipment. Hoisted on the forestay it can be used as an anchor light, or it can be used as a gangway light, a cabin light, a torch, a stern light to show should big ships come near, while suitably dimmed it can be used to illuminate the compass and chart table as well.

Washing paintwork, etc. Nothing is better or more effective for washing paint than a handful of washing soda in a bucket of warm water. The mixture is known as 'sugi-mugi' and is used in big ships the world over. The method is first to sponge over a large area and allow it a little while to get to work. Then rub the area more thoroughly and, with a different cloth, wash off with fresh water and dry. It is particularly good for shifting grease and, come to that, so are a few particles of soda in the washing-up water.

Water containers There is a lot to be said for using a battery of small plastic containers rather than building a proper watering tank in your boat. To begin with they cost nothing, and are easy to clean and sterilize whatever their former employment, or whoever your source of supply (use sodium metabisulphite as supplied from chemist shops for home wine-making enthusiasts). They are simple to stow and can be used to fill up any awkward

119

space; for example half a dozen can be placed under a bunk and fed to the galley by means of a pump. This provides you with a constant check for you can see at a glance or know by a vulgar sucking sound how many full ones are left. Another benefit is that they are light and easy to carry, a point that will be appreciated by those who have ever had occasion to hand aboard a heavy jerrycan from a dinghy. Indeed once you get into the habit of taking a handful of them ashore now and then – handing one each to all members of the family – the job of watering ship is much less of a chore.

They are much less of a problem too in places where there is no hose. For even a landlord or beach whelk-stall owner can hardly deny a request for one gallon (especially when it comes from a three-year-old child) whereas he would have a right to flinch at a jerrycan plonked on his counter.

Finally a battery of small containers that are continually emptied and changed ensures that your supply of water is constantly sweet and fresh, which is more than can be said for water left in some of the purpose-built tanks. Then, just to be sure, it's no trouble to take them home at the end of the season and rinse them with sodium what's-a-name again.

Whisker pole   A cheap whisker pole for booming out the genoa can be made by fixing a bolt, or hardwood dowel, together with a plywood disc, inside the end of a length of bamboo (Figure 38). To engage or disengage it is simply pulled away; no need to lean dangerously overboard to wrestle with snap shackle and flogging genoa. (The inboard end has an angled piece of rod which fits into the spinnaker ring like a gooseneck.)

Winches   One of the most expensive items of deck machinery is the winch, or rather a set of them since they seem to come in pairs. Indeed they proliferate and nowadays we see boats, even quite small boats, for which a pair of swivel clam cleats for the sheets would be perfectly adequate, sporting not only sheet winches, but halyard winches and centre plate winches, even

120

Figure 38

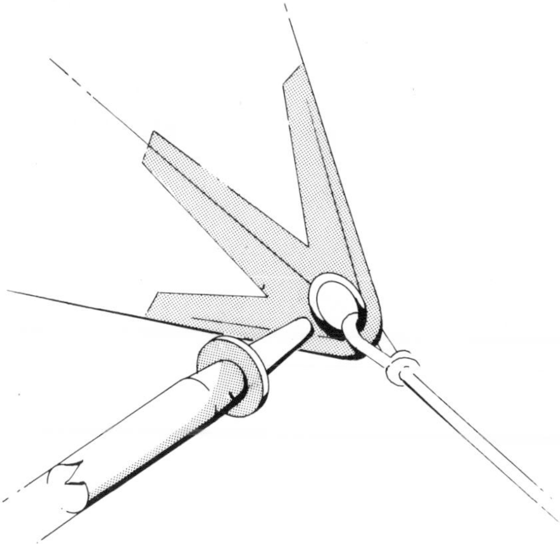

windlasses! Smaller boat and even large ones too, providing they don't carry huge genoas, can be handled quite safely without winches, all it takes is a little old-fashioned seamanship.

Begin with the headsail. Many would contend that a winch is essential to gather in the headsail but it is doubtful that Thames bargemen would agree. A fifty-ton barge with heavy flax sails could be put about without even one turn of a winch. The headsail was sheeted to an iron horse which ran across the deck and that way even the ship's cat could handle it. A sailing yacht too can be fitted with a horse or at least a boom foresail arrangement, usually in conjunction with a cutter rig.

A cutter doesn't really need to have winches. It can have a large sail area, even larger than a sloop's, but because this is made up of two sails the whole thing remains quite manageable. Going about from one tack to the other, the headsail is got in first quickly while the boat is luff to the wind. Then once this sail is sheeted home it is relatively easy to get the staysail in because it is blanketed by the headsail. Even less of a struggle with a boom staysail of course. There are also other ways of sheeting in the headsail by using the sheets to advantage and leading them as 'whips'. Figure 39 illustrates two methods.

121

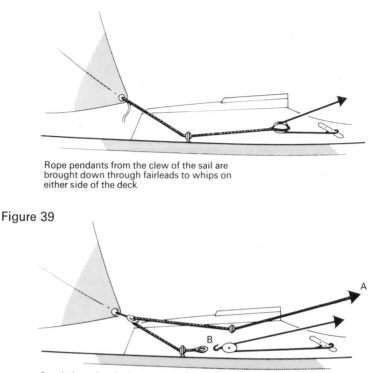

Rope pendants from the clew of the sail are
brought down through fairleads to whips on
either side of the deck

Figure 39

A variation whereby in strong winds an extra
purchase can be got by first making fast 'A' and
then hooking on at 'B'

One remarkable piece of improvisation is a DIY snubbing
winch (Figure 40) invented by Mr S. C. Hine and published in
Practical Boatowner some years ago. It is suitable for jib sheets
in boats up to about five tons and consists basically of a
bicycle freewheel sprocket and a drum turned from a piece of
2½ inch (65 mm) Tufnol rod. The freewheel mechanism is, says
the inventor, more than strong enough and certainly one only
has to recall cycling uphill standing on the pedals to have some
idea of its strength. Indeed he says if two freewheel ratchets
were clamped one on top of the other and fitted with a handle
then the whole thing could be made into a lever action winch
suitable for a six-tonner, although in this case a stout spindle
bolt would also be needed.

122

Figure 40

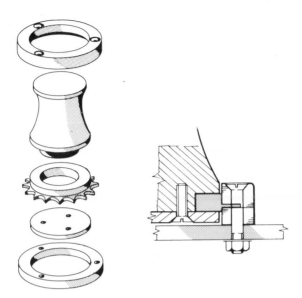

The drum has a short stem which is a push fit into the centre of the freewheel. It is held securely in place with a Tufnol disc clamped through from underneath, with three zero BA hexagon-headed brass screws tapped into the stem. The sprocket part of the freewheel is held rigid by a ring made from 12 mm plywood. This plywood has a rebate to accommodate the teeth of the sprocket and the three 2 BA screws which hold the ring down are arranged to pass between the teeth to prevent them from turning.

Mr Hine says he can usually manage to squirt some oil down through the cracks and in this way the sprocket can be kept rust-free for about four seasons. Still, as he points out, freewheels are very cheap and it's little bother to replace one. A small grease nipple could be fitted from underneath and fitted into one of the oiling holes.

But for all these suggestions, the reality is that most cruising boats today follow the racing fashion and derive most of their drive from the headsails. For the small cruiser owner and his wife it's a retrogression and leads to unnecessary heavy sail handling and sometimes dangerous foredeck work. However, this is a digression for the point is that, like them or not, big headsails need big winches . . . or at least *one* winch. A friend of mine with a 32-foot ketch has saved himself a considerable expense by fitting just one winch in the middle of the cockpit. It is mounted on a movable beam and is adaptable as was the old donkey winch in a sailing ship. That is to say not only does it handle both sets of sheets (with considerably more ease and comfort than with winches at the side of the cockpit) but also it takes care of the main and jib halyards: the ideal application for the single-hander!

In a small boat it is sometimes impossible to get the luff of the headsail taut simply by swinging on the halyard. However, there is no need to go to the expense of a winch when a simple tack tackle can do the job so easily. The ordinary manner of rigging them with the hauling part leading off the standing, or lower, block means that one-third of the power is being lost because the block is rigged to disadvantage. Sensibly then, rig

Figure 41

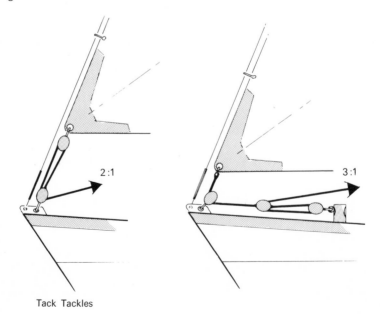

Tack Tackles

the tackle as shown in the drawing (Figure 41) with a lead block on the stem fitting. Tack tackles can also be rigged on the main boom to similar advantage.

Halyards can be set up hard with the swig hook (Figure 42) or shivver hitch (Figure 43). The latter is applied in conjunction with a small luff tackle permanently kept at the mast heel. From the top block there is a rope pendant rove through a small plywood disc. This acts as a stopper. The halyard is first made up hand tight and secured. Then the tackle and stopper is applied with a shivver hitch (start the same way as with a rolling hitch). This holds quite securely so that both hands are free to haul down on the tackle.

The cheapest winches on the market, and very strong and reliable they are too, are the range of Viking winches made by Southend Engineering Co. Ltd, High Street, Leigh-on-Sea, Essex.

Figure 42   Figure 43

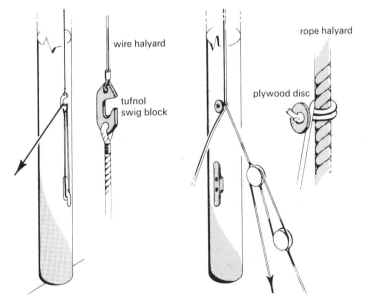

Tufnol swig block for setting up halyard   Shivver hitch, kept handy can be used for setting up halyard

Wind direction   The cheapest wind director is a flag.

Windows   Essex Aluminium of Southminster, Essex, usually have a large number of left-over windows that were ordered but never collected, or from firms that have gone bankrupt. They sell them off cheaply. Perhaps your local aluminium window manufacturer does also?

Yuloh   The yuloh method of single oar sculling used in China and Japan is faster and less strenuous than our own method. Instead of having to twist the blade as we do, the 'mechanism' of the yuloh does this automatically so that all that is necessary is a simple push-and-pull movement. It is fast; observers in Japan claim to have seen fishermen move 22-foot boats, which weigh at least a ton, at speeds of about four knots!

Mr K. Albury, a reader of *Yachting Monthly*, has adopted the yuloh principle to propel his 19 foot (5·7 m) boat but has considerably improved and modernized the fittings. Here, in his own words, is how he has done it:

'The parts required for my system are:

1. A $\frac{3}{4}$ inch (18 mm) ball on a $\frac{5}{16}$ inch (8 mm) stem. This a friend made for me in one piece in stainless steel.
2. A metal plate to retain the ball in the oar. This plate is curved to the curve of the loom of the oar and slotted to control the angle at which the blade will move through the water.
3. A plastic rowlock and socket.

'A hole is drilled in the shaft of the oar at the appropriate place and in line with the blade $\frac{3}{4}$ inch (18 mm) diameter and just deep enough to accommodate the ball. (I put some P38 filler treated with hardener into the hole, then pressed the greased ball into it to make a thrust surface. This has proved to be very satisfactory.) It will now be seen that if the stem of the ball is held rigid and with the oar on top, the oar will fall over the ball. The amount it will fall is governed by the length of the slot in the retaining plate. The slot is also made just

126

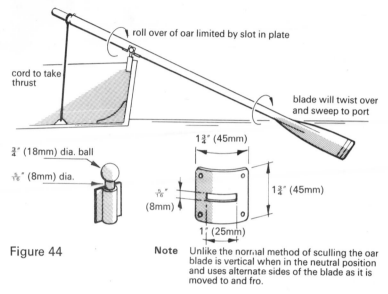

push to starboard – oar will roll over ball to starboard

roll over of oar limited by slot in plate

cord to take thrust

blade will twist over and sweep to port

$\frac{3}{4}$" (18mm) dia. ball

$\frac{5}{16}$" (8mm) dia.

$1\frac{3}{4}$" (45mm)

$\frac{5}{16}$" (8mm)

$1\frac{3}{4}$" (45mm)

1" (25mm)

Figure 44

Note Unlike the normal method of sculling the oar blade is vertical when in the neutral position and uses alternate sides of the blade as it is moved to and fro.

sufficiently wide to allow the blade to be lifted clear of the water. With the ball in place in the oar, the retaining plate is fitted by four screws so that the stem of the ball lies centrally in the slot but at an angle to allow the blade to be fully immersed in the water. (This will depend on the height of the transom and the length of the oar. I am using an 8 foot (2·3 m) oar on my Hunter 19, but a longer one would probably be even better.)

'The socket of the rowlock is fitted as convenient in the transom. The arms of the rowlock are cut off and a hole is drilled in the body to take the stem of the ball – a tight fit is best – deep enough to leave about $\frac{5}{8}$ inch of stem clear. The ball assembly stays on the oar and just needs to be dropped into the transom socket.

'A cord is dropped from the handle of the oar to a suitable location to fix the depth of the blade finally and to help take the thrust. Now all one has to do is to push and pull the handle of the oar away and back and the oar will do the rest – no skill required, steering is easy – it's all so simple! I have been using it for two seasons so it has been well tried.'